"It has been obvious that religion influences our politics, but what John Fea understands is that politics has had a major influence on Christianity. In *Believe Me*, Fea takes evangelicalism seriously, treating it with the honest respect it deserves. He also manages to help us understand American politics in a much clearer way that will not only help us process the past, but chart our course forward. I highly recommend this book to all who remain confounded by the state of faith and politics today."

— Michael Wear
author of *Reclaiming Hope: Lessons Learned in the Obama White House about the Future of Faith in America*

"John Fea's timely and sobering book convincingly shows how legitimate concerns from white evangelical Protestants about a rapidly secularizing American culture metastasized into a fear-driven brew of half-truths, fanciful nostalgia, misplaced Christian nationalism, ethical hypocrisy, and political naiveté—precisely, that is, the mix that led so many white evangelicals not only to cast their votes for Donald Trump, but to regard him as a literal godsend."

— Mark Noll
author of *The Scandal of the Evangelical Mind*

"It would be enough for John Fea to marshal his considerable prowess as a historian in proving how evangelicals have been propelled by fear, nostalgia, and the pursuit of power, as he does so compellingly in this book. But he also speaks here as a theologian and an evangelical himself, eloquently pointing toward a better gospel way. This is a call to action for evangelicals to move beyond the politics of fear to become a 'faithful presence' in a changing world."

— Jana Riess
senior columnist for *Religion News Service*

"While the significant support for Donald Trump by white evangelicals has been the stuff of headlines, there has been little serious probing of the deeper factors at work. John Fea now gives us what we need, with his insightful tracing here of the theological-spiritual road that has brought us to this point. A wise and important book!"

— Richard Mouw
author of *Uncommon Decency*

"For those who think the embrace of Trump by the 'Court Evangelicals' might be an example of yielding to the political temptation that Jesus resisted, this is the book to read. Noted evangelical historian John Fea provides a thoughtful and engaging account and critique of how this unlikely alliance came to be."

— George Marsden
author of *Religion and American Culture*

BELIEVE ME

The Evangelical Road
to Donald Trump

John Fea

WILLIAM B. EERDMANS PUBLISHING COMPANY
GRAND RAPIDS, MICHIGAN

Wm. B. Eerdmans Publishing Co.
4035 Park East Court SE, Grand Rapids, MI 49546
www.eerdmans.com

Hardcover edition 2018
Paperback edition 2020

Printed in the United States of America

26 25 24 23 22 21 20   1 2 3 4 5 6 7

ISBN 978-0-8028-7742-0

Library of Congress Cataloging-in-Publication Data

Names: Fea, John, author.
Title: Believe me : the Evangelical road to Donald Trump / John Fea.
Description: Grand Rapids : Eerdmans Publishing Co., 2018. |
    Includes bibliographical references and index.
Identifiers: LCCN 2018007625 | ISBN 9780802877420
    (pbk. : alk. paper)
Subjects: LCSH: Christianity and politics—United States. |
    Evangelicalism. | Trump, Donald, 1946- | Voting—Religious aspects—
    Christianity. | Christians—Political activity—United States.
Classification: LCC BR516 .F425 2018 | DDC 277.3/083—dc23
    LC record available at https://lccn.loc.gov/2018007625

To the 19 percent

CONTENTS

ACKNOWLEDGMENTS

I want to thank the administration of Messiah College for the time and resources provided me to write and think about the connections between American history, religion and politics. The good folks at Eerdmans Publishing—Anita Eerdmans, James Ernest, and especially David Bratt—have been nothing but encouraging and helpful from the moment I first brought this project to them. My conversations with David have shaped this work more than he will ever know. A very big thank you goes to Devon Hearn, my research assistant. Devon has done the unheralded work of tracking down sources, requesting books through InterLibrary loan, and taking on tasks that have enabled me to write under a tight deadline. And she does it all with a smile on her face! Collin Gallagher, who graciously volunteered to help with this book, proved to be an excellent undergraduate researcher. Alanna Carnes, Robin Schwarzmann, and Kyra Yoder helped with the proofreading. I also want to thank Phillip Luke Sinitiere for taking time out of his Advent season to provide comments on several chapters, and Caroline Fea for offering comments on the introduction and the conclusion. As always, I could not have written this book without the loving support and regular encouragement of Joy, Allyson, and Caroline.

INTRODUCTION

On August 6, 2015, the night of the first Republican presidential primary debate, what would become one of the most extraordinary presidential campaigns in American history faced an unsurprising moment—that is, highly unusual in most of the industrialized world but unsurprising in Republican politics. After two hours of debate, a Facebook user named Chase A. Norton asked one of the last questions of the evening: "I want to know if any [of the debaters] have received a word from God on what they should do and take care of first." Three of the candidates, Texas senator Ted Cruz, Wisconsin governor Scott Walker, and Florida senator Marco Rubio, jumped on what seemed like a golden opportunity to appeal to white evangelical voters. Cruz reminded the audience that God speaks to him through the Bible and told the story about his father "giving his heart to Jesus." Walker said he was "redeemed from his sins" by "the blood of Jesus Christ" and would thus seek to do "His will" as president. Rubio talked about "God's blessing" on the American people. The message to conservative evangelical voters was strong and clear: "I am one of you!"

New York real-estate tycoon and reality-television star Donald Trump, whose double-digit lead in the polls had secured him a spot at the center of the stage, was not asked to answer Norton's question. But after watching the other candidates' efforts to claim the evangelical high ground, his campaign must have realized that, if he could not make a similar appeal to white evangelical voters, he would not be at center stage for very long. Trump would need to find his evangelical groove.

Coincidentally, I had spent the morning of that debate rereading University of Virginia sociologist James Davison Hunter's manifesto *To Change the World: The Irony, Tragedy, and Possibility of Christianity in America* (2010). Hunter argues that evangelical Christian attempts to "change the world" through politics—electing the right candidates, who will then pass the right laws and approve the right justices for the Supreme Court—have largely failed. In grasping for political power, Hunter says, evangelicals have made it more difficult to spread the gospel, promote justice for the poor and oppressed, and pursue human flourishing in the places where God has called and placed them. In one of the more telling and prophetic passages of the book, he writes: "The proclivity toward domination and toward the politicization of everything leads Christianity today to bizarre turns, turns that . . . transform much of the Christian public witness into the very opposite of the witness Christianity is supposed to offer." Christians were never meant to change this world; instead, they are called to "honor the creator of all goodness, beauty, and truth, a manifestation of our loving obedience to God, and a fulfillment of God's command to love our neighbor." Hunter urges evangelical Christians to stop fighting the culture wars and pursue a course of "faithful presence" in their local communities and neighborhoods.[1]

Introduction

I read Hunter's book and watched the debate, not just as a historian interested in the relationship between religion and politics, but as a participant. I have long identified with the label *evangelical*: I attend an evangelical church, and I am a professor at a college with deep roots in the evangelical tradition. Of course, that deceptively simple label refers to a movement with a surprisingly diverse set of subcultures, and I have plenty of disagreements with those within those subcultures. But for all of the complexity behind the word "evangelical," at its heart is a simple and compelling notion: *evangel*, or "good news."

Over the course of the next several months Donald Trump made what seemed to be awkward attempts to win over white evangelicals. At times, his efforts to connect with and understand a religious culture he knew nothing about were comical. In a speech at Liberty University he referred to Saint Paul's Second Epistle to the Corinthians as "Two Corinthians" (Americans who study the Bible say "Second Corinthians"). In an interview in Ames, Iowa, he claimed that he never asks God for forgiveness, and he referred to Holy Communion as drinking "my little wine" and having "my little cracker." (Trump's self-proclaimed knowledge of the meaning of the sacrament did not prevent him from nearly placing a few bucks in the communion plate during a worship service in Iowa.)[2] He was apt to show up at campaign rallies clutching an old family Bible. When asked what his favorite Bible verse was, he said he liked "an eye for an eye," a reference to the Old Testament punishment system set forth in Exodus 21:22-25. (Trump was obviously not aware that Jesus himself, in Matthew 5:38-39, had something to say about the Exodus passage: "You have heard that it was said 'An eye for an eye, and a tooth for a tooth.' But I tell you, do not resist an evil person. If anyone slaps you on the right cheek, turn to him the other cheek also.")

3

Beyond those bumbling attempts to use evangelical language, Trump's decidedly un-Christian behavior on the campaign trail seemed at first blush to reinforce the challenge he might face in wooing evangelicals. On more than one occasion—during his rants on topics ranging from Megyn Kelly's debate questions to Carly Fiorina's and Heidi Cruz's physical appearance—Trump denigrated women. He used the televised debates to belittle his political opponents with junior-high nicknames, and he even bragged about the size of his genitals. He claimed that the father of one of his opponents was involved in the Kennedy assassination. He announced that another competitor had a "pathological temper" and was not a member of a real Christian denomination. He denigrated a war hero and former presidential candidate. After the release of a tape on which he talked about the ways he used his celebrity to sexually assault women, the 2016 GOP presidential nominee dismissed his language as mere "locker-room talk." Within hours, multiple women came forward to confirm that what Trump bragged about to an entertainment reporter was more than just locker-room talk. It was quite real.

Ironically, somewhere between the comical religious blunders and the release of the reports of sexual assault, Trump managed to convince many evangelicals that he was a Christian. It was clear evidence of his skills as a politician. Prior to his decision to run for office, very few Americans, including American evangelicals, were even aware that he was anything but a profane man—a playboy and adulterer who worshiped, not at the throne of God, but at the throne of Mammon. Trump's ability to win over evangelicals is illustrated in a January 2018 CNN interview with a group of female Trump supporters in the wake of news that his lawyer had paid $130,000 dollars to silence a porn star with whom he had had an adulterous affair. One woman said that Trump deserved forgiveness because he had "accepted Christ" into his "heart and life" and "asked forgiveness of his sins." (These women said nothing about Melania Trump—the woman who most likely experienced pain and embarrassment from Trump's past sins).[3]

Nothing Trump could say or do would deter his diehard white evangelical supporters. This is still the case. Most evangelicals were willing to ignore his moral lapses because he had, to their way of thinking, the correct policy proposals. Trump promised to place a conservative on the Supreme Court, to build a wall along the southern border (and have Mexico pay for it), to protect white Americans from all the "rapists" who were illegally streaming across the border; he also promised to round up undocumented immigrants and kick them out of the country—even if it meant dividing families. He assured his evangelical base that he would prevent Muslims from entering the United States, would "bomb the hell" out of ISIS, and would bring an end to the Affordable Care Act. Furthermore, he would defend "religious freedom" by repealing the part of the IRS code that prevents churches from endorsing political candidates (the so-called Johnson Amendment), would pursue an "America first" foreign policy, would move the location of the American embassy in Israel from Tel Aviv to Jerusalem, and would pull the United States out of the Paris climate agreements. Trump would "make America great again."

As the campaign went on, it became clear that many more evangelicals preferred Trump's candidacy to James Davison Hunter's advice. Instead of Hunter's "faithful presence," we all witnessed, once again, evangelicals reaching for political power. On November 8, 2016, 81 percent of self-described white evangelicals helped vote Donald Trump into the White

House. A higher percentage of evangelicals voted for Trump than did for George W. Bush in 2000 and 2004, John McCain in 2008, and Mitt Romney in 2012.[4]

Like most people, I sat down early Tuesday evening to watch election returns fully expecting that, by the time I went to bed, Hillary Clinton would be declared the country's first female president. Instead, I saw my home state of Pennsylvania fall to Trump, followed by the Clinton "firewall" states of Michigan and Wisconsin. I was shocked. I was saddened. I was angry. But my emotions were less about the new president-elect and more about the large number of my fellow evangelicals who voted for him.

Five days later—the Lord's Day—I took my seat in the sanctuary of the central Pennsylvania megachurch where I have worshiped for the last sixteen years. As I looked around at my fellow worshipers, I could not help thinking that there was a strong possibility, if the reports and polls were correct, that eight out of every ten people in that sanctuary—my brothers and sisters in my community of faith—had voted for the new president-elect. This seemed to reflect deep divisions in how we understand the world, and it was deeply distressing.

Over time, my distress did not wane, but my surprise did. As a historian studying religion and politics, I should have seen this coming. This election, while certainly unique and unprecedented in American history, is also the latest manifestation of a long-standing evangelical approach to public life. This political playbook was written in the 1970s and drew heavily from an even longer history of white evangelical fear. It is a playbook characterized by attempts to "win back" or "restore the culture." It is a playbook grounded in a highly problematic interpretation of the relationship between Christianity and the American founding. It is playbook that too often gravitates toward nativism, xenophobia, racism, intolerance, and an unbiblical view of American exceptionalism. It is a playbook that divides rather than unites. This playbook survived its greatest test in the election of 2016.

This book is my attempt to make sense of it all. I approach this subject not as a political scientist, pollster, or pundit, but as a historian who identifies as an evangelical Christian. For too long, white evangelical Christians have engaged in public life through a strategy defined by the politics of fear, the pursuit of worldly power, and a nostalgic longing for a national past that may have never existed in the first place. Fear. Power. Nostalgia. These ideas are at the heart of this book, and I believe that they best explain that 81 percent.

The first three chapters work backward from the election of 2016 to identify some of the reasons why white evangelicals in America have been so afraid. Chapter 1 explores the 2016 GOP primary and attempts to explain why evangelical Republican voters chose Donald Trump over other more traditional Christian Right candidates such as Cruz, Rubio, and Walker. The social and cultural changes of the Obama presidency—particularly regarding human sexuality—happened so quickly that conservative Christians had very little time to process what they believed to be an erosion of the moral foundations of their nation. In this state of panic, evangelicals saw Trump as a strongman who would protect them from the forces working to undermine the values of the world they once knew. The cultural shifts of the Obama administration represented the latest—and perhaps the final—chapter in what pollster Robert P. Jones has described as the "end of white Christian America."[5]

Chapter 2 places the 2016 general election contest between Donald Trump and Hillary Clinton in the context of the political playbook forged by Jerry Falwell and the Moral Majority in the 1970s. The roots of evangelical support for Donald Trump go much deeper than simply the last eight or nine years. Ever since World War II, white evangelicals have waged a desperate and largely failing war against the thickening walls of separation between church and state, the removal of Christianity from public schools, the growing ethnic and religious diversity of the country, the intrusion of the federal government into their everyday lives (especially as it pertains to desegregation and civil rights), and legalized abortion. Chapter 3 pushes this history of fear even deeper into the American experience. The postwar anxiety was the logical result of three hundred years—from the Puritans to the American Revolution, and from nativism to fundamentalism—of evangelical fears about the direction in which their "Christian nation" was moving. Despite God's commands to trust him in times of despair, evangelicals have always been very fearful people, and they have built their understanding of political engagement around the anxiety they have felt amid times of social and cultural change.

Chapter 4 describes the men and women I have identified as the "court evangelicals." The politics of fear inevitably results in a quest for power. Political influence, many evangelicals believe, is the only way to restore the nation to the moral character of its founding. How much time and money has been spent seeking political power when such resources might have been invested more effectively in pursuing a course of faithful presence! Clergymen and religious leaders have, at least since Billy Graham, regularly visited the White House to advise the president. Like the members of the kings' courts during the late Middle Ages and the Renaissance, who sought influence and worldly approval by flattering the monarch rather than prophetically speaking truth to power, Trump's court evangelicals boast about their "unprecedented access" to the White House and exalt the president for his faith-friendly policies.

Finally, evangelical support for Donald Trump is rooted in nostalgia for a bygone Christian golden age. Chapter 5 takes a critical look at the way conservative evangelicals have used the past in their efforts to build a case for Trump. The belief that the United States was founded as, and continues to be, a Christian nation (a view I occasionally describe in this book as "Christian nationalism") undergirds much of evangelical politics today. The late historian and cultural critic Christopher Lasch has written: "Nostalgia freezes the past in images of timeless, childlike innocence."[6] It fails to recognize change over time. So, instead of doing the hard work necessary for engaging a more diverse society with the claims of Christian orthodoxy, evangelicals have become intellectually lazy, preferring to respond to cultural change by trying to reclaim a world that is rapidly disappearing and has little chance of ever coming back. This backward-looking approach to politics can be seen no more clearly than in the evangelicals' embrace of Trump's campaign slogan: "Make America great again."

In exploring all of this, I speak as a historian, of course. For me, however, that's not enough. I want to explore alternatives to the fear, the search for power, and the nostalgia. How do we reconcile the white evangelical politics of fear with the scriptural command to "fear not"? Novelist and essayist Marilynne Robinson has said that "fear is not a Christian habit of mind."[7] Christian Scripture makes it clear that the strongman who delivers is not Donald Trump, but the God who promises to be a refuge and strength, a very present help in times of trouble (Ps. 46:1–2). What would it take to replace fear with Christian hope?

The court evangelicals have been shown "all the kingdoms of the world and their glory" (Matt. 4:8–10); but, unlike Jesus in his encounter with the Tempter, they have gladly embraced them. Evangelicals claim to follow a Savior who relinquished worldly power—even to the point of giving his life. Yet they continue to place their hope in political candidates as a means of advancing an agenda that confuses the kingdom of God with the United States of America. Evangelicals often decry the idea of "separation of church and state" (although, as we will see in chapter 2, they have not always thought this way), but this constitutional principle has always served as a safeguard to protect the church from the temptations that come with worldly power. Political scientist Glenn Tinder says that power is a "morally problematic" idea because it almost always induces "others to serve one's own purposes." In the sense that political power objectifies other human beings, it is a "degraded relationship if judged by the standards of love."[8] Political power does not have to result in immoral ends, but it nearly always does due to the fallenness of human beings and the brokenness of a world stained by sin. Humility, on the other hand, is always centered on the cross of Jesus Christ, a political act that ushered in a new kind of political entity— the kingdom of God. Humility thus requires listening, debate, conversation, and dialogue that respects the dignity of all of God's human creation. What would it take to replace the pursuit of power with humility?

Evangelicals' propensity for nostalgia makes them susceptible to a political candidate who wants to "make America great *again.*" Trump's famous slogan is, at its core, a historical one: it assumes that there was a moment in the American past that was indeed "great." Of course, national "greatness" is often in the eye of the beholder. A bygone era that may have been great for one group of people may have been oppressive for others. Since Trump rarely says specifically which era in the American past he thinks was great, we can only measure his understanding of greatness through the moments in American history that he regularly invokes. Sadly, whenever Trump turns to the past, he usually alludes to some of the nation's darkest moments. He looks back fondly on those times in American life when our leaders sought divisiveness over the common good and discrimination over the celebration of diversity grounded in human dignity. Such an approach to "making America great again" is deeply problematic for those who claim to be followers of Jesus Christ. What would it take to replace nostalgia with history?

When Donald Trump speaks to his followers in the mass rallies that have now become a fixture of his populist brand, he loves to use the phrase "believe me." The Internet is filled with video montages of Trump using this signature catch phrase even more frequently than "make America great again":

"Believe me, folks, we're building the wall, believe me, believe me, we're building the wall."

"I love women. Believe me, I love women. I love women. And you know what else, I have great respect for women, believe me."

"I am the least, the least racist person that you've ever met, believe me."[9]

"The world is in trouble, but we're going to straighten it out, okay? That's what I do. I fix things. We're going to straighten it out, believe me."[10]

And, perhaps most importantly:

"So let me state this right up front: [in] a Trump administration our Christian heritage will be cherished, protected, defended—like you've never seen before. Believe me."[11]

This book is the story of why so many American evangelicals *believe* in Donald Trump.

CHAPTER 1

THE EVANGELICAL POLITICS OF FEAR

Fear's a dangerous thing. It can turn your heart black, you can trust. It'll take your God-filled soul and fill it with devils and dust.

— Bruce Springsteen

W hen Donald Trump rode down the escalator at Trump Tower on June 16, 2015, to announce his candidacy for president of the United States, few thought the real-estate-magnate-turned-reality-television-star had a chance. Even fewer could have predicted the support he would win among white evangelical Christians. The last half-century has taught us that evangelical voters prefer elected officials who at least try to present themselves as men and women of character. Trump's moral indiscretions and playboy lifestyle should have disqualified him among these guardians of evangelical morality. Yet, just over thirteen months later, Trump was at the Republican National Convention in Cleveland accepting the GOP nomination. What happened?

Trump's appeal to evangelical voters during the 2016 Republican primaries continues to baffle political commentators. How did a crude-talking, thrice-married, self-proclaimed philanderer and ultra-materialistic businessman who showed virtually no evidence of a Spirit-filled life win over evangelicals in a field of qualified GOP candidates who self-identified—in one way or another—with this form of conservative Christianity?

Why, for example, did evangelical voters shun Mike Huckabee, a Southern Baptist pastor, or Rick Santorum, a self-described "evangelical Catholic," whom *Time* magazine once included on its list of the "25 Most Influential Evangelicals in America"? Both men won large numbers of evangelical votes after impressive showings in the Iowa caucuses of 2008 and 2012, respectively, and both had proven that they could carry a significant portion of Southern states. Or why not retired brain surgeon Ben Carson? The popular author of best-selling Christian memoirs had become a viable presidential candidate following a 2013 speech at the National Prayer Breakfast in which he criticized the policies of Barack Obama (with Obama seated a few feet to his right) and defended the idea of "tithing" as a model for the nation's tax policy.

As the primary season of 2016 progressed, the evangelical candidates with the best chance to win the GOP nomination were Florida senator Marco Rubio, a Catholic who attended a large Southern Baptist church, and a Cuban-born preacher's son, Ted Cruz, who rode evangelical support to a Senate seat from Texas. Nor did the evangelical parade of presidential candidates stop there. Ohio governor John Kasich, Wisconsin governor Scott Walker, Louisiana governor Bobby Jindal, former Florida governor Jeb Bush, and businesswoman Carly Fiorina—all seemed to be men and women of character, and they all had positions on social issues that made them appealing to evangelical voters.[1]

Furthermore, these candidates understood the political commitments of conservative evangelicals. Some of them would even feel comfortable preaching a sermon in an evangelical church or comforting people using the words of Scripture. But what gave them a legitimate shot at the GOP nomination was their ability to engage in the politics of fear. To win the evangelical vote, these political candidates knew that they would have to convince the faithful that the Christian fabric of the country was unraveling, the nation's evangelical moorings were loosening, and the barbarians were amassing at the borders—ready for a violent takeover. Fear is the political language conservative evangelicals know best.

The Politics of Fear

Fear has been a staple of American politics since the founding of the republic. In 1800, the *Connecticut Courant*, a Federalist newspaper that supported President John Adams in his reelection campaign against Thomas Jefferson, suggested that, if the Electoral College chose Jefferson, the founding father and religious skeptic from Virginia, the country would have to deal with a wave of murder, atheism, rape, adultery, and robbery.[2] In the 1850s, the anti-Catholic and anti-immigration American Party, commonly known as the "Know-Nothing Party," was infamous for its American-flag banner emblazoned with the words "Native Americans: Beware of Foreign Influence."

In modern America, campaign ads keep us in a constant state of fear—and not always from right-wing sources either. I still get a shiver up my spine when I watch "Daisy Girl," the

1964 Lyndon Johnson campaign advertisement that opens with a little girl standing in a quiet meadow picking the petals off a daisy. Midway through the ad, an ominous countdown begins, and the camera zooms into the girl's eye, where we the viewers see the mushroom cloud of a nuclear explosion. As the ad closes, we hear the voice of sportscaster Chris Schenkel reading the following words on the screen: "Vote for President Johnson on November 3rd. . . . The stakes are too high for you to stay home." This ad played an important role in Johnson's landslide victory over his Republican opponent, Barry Goldwater, the conservative Arizona senator who had made reckless statements about the use of nuclear weapons.[3] Fear is a powerful political tool.

Political fear is so dangerous because it usually stems from legitimate concerns shared by a significant portion of the voting population. Thomas Jefferson *did* oppose government-sponsored religion, and he *did* question many supernatural elements in the Bible. Barry Goldwater *did* support the use of atomic weapons in Vietnam. Today the growing number of Muslims living in the United States *does* raise important questions about how religious identity intersects with American values, or how we should defend the religious liberty of the millions of peaceful Muslims while still protecting Americans from the threat of murderous Islamic terror groups. The United States *does* have a problem with undocumented immigrants entering the country illegally. And it is clear that television and social media make it easier for politicians to define our fears for us. They take these legitimate concerns, as political theorist Corey Robin puts it, and transform them "into imminent threats."

Jason Bivins has noted, in his study of religious fear, that "moral panics" tend to "rely on presumptions more than facts;

they dramatize and sensationalize so as to keep audiences in a state of continual alertness." For example, studies have shown that during the 1990s, two-thirds of Americans believed that the national crime rate was *rising*, even though it was actually *dropping*. Donald Trump himself, during his 2016 campaign, exploited this fear by claiming that crime was rising when it was actually falling. He attempted to portray refugees and undocumented immigrants as threats to the American public even though the chance that an American will die at the hands of a refugee terrorist is about one in 3.6 million; the chance of being murdered by an undocumented immigrant is one in 10.9 million per year. One is more likely to die from walking across a railroad track or having one's clothes spontaneously catch fire. Yet Trump has managed to convince Americans that immigrants are "imminent threats" to their safety. He rode this wave of fear all the way to the White House, and it continues to serve as the foundation for an immigration policy that revolves around the construction of a massive border wall between the United States and Mexico.[4]

The "Pizzagate" conspiracy theory during the 2016 presidential election is another example of fear-mongering. When Wikileaks released the hacked emails of Hillary Clinton's campaign manager, John Podesta, anti-Clinton social-media sites claimed that certain words in the emails were code for a child-sex ring sponsored by the Democratic Party and operated out of Comet Ping-Pong, a Washington DC pizzeria. A North Carolina man who claimed he was "investigating Pizzagate" came to Washington with an assault rifle and fired three shots into the restaurant. Thankfully, no one was killed or injured in the shooting. The event became an example of how a sense of fear built on false information and innuendo could place human lives in jeopardy.[5]

Barack Hussein Obama

Barack Obama became the perfect foil for the evangelical purveyors of the politics of fear. Obama was an exotic figure to many white conservative Christians, and he represented nearly everything that made white evangelicals afraid: he grew up in Hawaii and spent time as a child in a predominantly Muslim country; he was the son of a white woman and a black man; he not only had a strange name, but he had the same middle name as a well-known Muslim dictator whom the United States had waged war against. Obama's embrace of Christianity took place in a liberal African American congregation with a pastor who was not shy about calling America to task for its past sins. But most importantly, Obama embraced policies on a host of social issues that alienated him almost immediately from most American evangelicals.

Obama's biracialism, single-parent upbringing, and global experiences made him a poster child for the demographic changes taking place in the country. He represented an American future that most white evangelicals were not yet willing to accept. The conservative evangelical assault on Obama began with the so-called birther controversy. In 2008, Roy Moore, the chief justice of the Alabama Supreme Court and a candidate, in December 2017, for an Alabama Senate seat (which he lost by only a narrow margin), was one of the first prominent Americans to claim that Obama was unqualified for the presidency because he was not born in the United States. Donald Trump brought the claims of Moore and others into the national spotlight.[6] As he contemplated a presidential run in 2012, Trump stoked fears that Obama was not an American citizen; he even claimed that he had hired private investigators to prove the claim he and Moore had made.

The place of Obama's birth—and the question of whether he was a United States citizen—became a major political talking point for Republicans, a party in which 45 percent of registered voters identified as "born again" or "evangelical." Politicians such as Mike Huckabee, Michelle Bachman, and Sarah Palin raised the birther issue in public interviews. The strategy seems to have worked on a long-term basis: in July 2017, eight months after the election of Donald Trump, an NBC News poll found that 72 percent of registered Republican voters *still* doubted Obama's citizenship.[7]

Others went even further in their criticism of Obama. Dinesh D'Souza, a conservative pundit who attended an evangelical megachurch and served as president of an evangelical Christian college, suggested that Obama was channeling his father's "socialist" and "anticolonial ambitions" in an effort to undermine the American way of life. Former speaker of the House Newt Gingrich, a favorite among many conservative evangelicals and a politician who had his own presidential ambitions in 2012, said that D'Souza had had a "stunning insight." Gingrich claimed that the best way to understand the Obama presidency was through a study of his father's "Kenyan anticolonial behavior."[8]

Many evangelical voters also believed that Obama was a Muslim, and American evangelicals have always feared Muslims. Jonathan Edwards, the patron saint of many modern-day evangelicals, believed Islam was one of "two great kingdoms which the devil . . . erected in opposition to the kingdom of Christ" (Catholicism was the other one). And the September 11, 2001, terrorist attacks exacerbated those fears. During Obama's political rise, and in his first term as president, anonymous chain emails circulated throughout the United States claiming that he attended a radical Islamic school in Indonesia, was the Antichrist prophesied in the New Testament book of Revelation, and swore upon a copy of the Koran when he took his oath of office for the United States Senate. A 2015 CNN poll found that nearly 30 percent of Americans and 43 percent of Republicans believed that the forty-fourth president was a Muslim.[9] Several prominent evangelicals suggested that Obama's family connection to Islam was one of the reasons he did not fight the Islamic State of Iraq and the Levant (ISIL) as strongly as many Americans hoped he would. Franklin Graham, the son of evangelist Billy Graham, said that Obama had "given a pass to Islam" in the war on terror because his father was a Muslim and his mother was "married to a Muslim." Richard Land, the retired president of the Ethics and Religious Liberty Commission of the Southern Baptist Church, said that Obama had "his head in the ground" and was living in an "alternative universe" in the battle against "radical Islamic jihadism."[10]

It is ludicrous to assume that Barack Obama is a Muslim. He is a Christian. During his campaign in 2008 and his ensuing presidency, he described himself—and was described by others—as a man of prayer who seeks the wisdom of the Christian God. He even has a story of personal conversion. On numerous occasions Obama said that his Christian faith provided strength in times of personal and national struggle and motivated him as a leader. During his presidency he repeatedly urged his fellow Americans, using New Testament language, to love one another as neighbors and, on at least one occasion, said that he wanted to work with his fellow believers to build "the kingdom of God here on earth." Obama regularly alluded to the words of Jesus Christ in his speeches, and once he told a National Prayer Breakfast audience that he relies on the Holy Spirit for spiritual guidance. His eulogy for

Rev. Clementa Pinckney, the minister killed in the deadly June 2015 shooting in an African American church in Charleston, South Carolina, may be the greatest pastor-in-chief moment since Abraham Lincoln's Second Inaugural Address in March 1865. In that speech Obama talked about the Christian concept of grace with remarkable nuance, even ending with an unaccompanied singing of the first verse of "Amazing Grace" before a delighted audience. Americans can debate whether Obama delivered on his faith-based promises, or whether he is the best model of a Christian statesman, but it is hard to deny, based on any verifiable information, that he is a follower of Jesus Christ.[11]

Other evangelicals were concerned about the *form* of Christianity that Barack Obama and his family embraced. In 1992, during his years as a community organizer in Chicago, Obama joined Trinity United Church of Christ, where the pastor, Rev. Jeremiah Wright, officiated at his wedding and the baptism of his two daughters. Trinity Church is a member of the United Church of Christ, a liberal denomination of the Protestant mainline that most evangelicals believe to be insufficiently orthodox and to be connected to a social Christianity that privileges acts of social justice over evangelism or the pursuit of personal piety. (For example, Trinity's doctrinal statement does not even mention the Bible).[12] Obama's commitment to Christianity would thus never satisfy most conservative evangelicals despite his willingness to freely talk about his faith at gatherings sponsored by the evangelical social-justice ministry Sojourners, the evangelical Messiah College, and Saddleback Church, the California megachurch whose pastor is the best-selling author Rick Warren.

During Obama's presidential run in 2007–2008, journalists uncovered several Wright sermons, preached in the wake of the September 11 attacks, that were critical of America's past treatment of Native Americans and African Americans, and that railed against the nation's imperialist foreign policy. When Wright quoted Malcolm X as saying "the chickens are coming home to roost" (a phrase Malcolm uttered to explain the "culture of hate" that led to the assassination of John F. Kennedy), many white Americans thought Wright was saying that the country deserved the September 11 attacks as punishment for its morally questionable past. By calling attention to the darker moments in American history, Wright was preaching a prophetic Christianity that was deeply rooted in the African American experience, which made clear the distinctions between the kingdom of God and the kingdom of the United States. For evangelicals who believe that the United States is a Christian country—an exceptional nation blessed by God above all others—these sermons went too far. Patriotic Christians condemned Wright and, by extension, his most famous parishioner. Obama did his best to disassociate himself from the remarks of his longtime pastor; after all, his presidential hopes were on the line. He tried to calm fears with a speech on race at the National Constitution Center in Philadelphia, but many evangelicals could not forget his connection to Rev. Wright. To most evangelicals, Barack Obama simply was not one of them.

By the time Obama took office, many white evangelicals believed he was not an American citizen, was a theological liberal at best and more likely a Muslim, and was affiliated with a radical African American community that hated the United States. But it was his social policies that they feared the most. Obama would win 24 percent of the white evangelical vote in 2008 and only 21 percent in 2012. His views on social issues would make it impossible to win more.[13]

Though he did not make it an important part of his presidential campaigns in either 2008 or 2012, Obama was decidedly in favor of legalized abortion, and he pledged his support to the Democratic Party's pro-choice platform. When evangelical pro-lifer Rick Warren asked him at what point a "baby gets human rights," he responded: "Whether you're looking at it from a theological perspective or a scientific perspective, answering that question with specificity is above my pay grade." Later in that conversation at Warren's Saddleback Church, Obama affirmed the right of women to choose to have an abortion "in consultation with their pastors or their spouses or their doctors or their family members."[14] His views on this issue were more progressive than the preceding Democratic president, Bill Clinton, who famously said that abortions should be "safe, legal, and rare." Obama had a strong record on a host of other issues regarding protection of vulnerable members of society—what might be called legitimate "life" issues—but for most conservative evangelicals, none of those issues contributes as much to their understanding of what it means to be "pro-life" as the more clear-cut issue of abortion. Evangelical social critic Ronald Sider has said that too many evangelicals believe "life begins at conception and ends at birth."[15]

Obama's pro-choice views informed evangelical opposition to the Affordable Care Act (known as Obamacare), his plan for universal health care. Many evangelicals worried—along with other free-market conservatives and libertarians—that Obamacare was an intrusion on their liberties and their right to choose their own health care options; but the strongest evangelical critique of the plan came from abortion opponents. Pro-life evangelicals joined forces with the United States Conference of Catholic Bishops, who opposed Obamacare because it required employers, even religious employers, to provide coverage for preventive care that included abortion-inducing contraceptives. The contraceptive mandate made the opposition to Obamacare an issue of religious liberty. In *Burwell v. Hobby Lobby* (2014), evangelicals won a victory when the Supreme Court decided that "for-profit closely held corporations" were exempt from providing contraceptives to their employees.

In the wake of *Burwell v. Hobby Lobby*, several religious organizations sued the federal government in the hopes of gaining their own exemptions from the contraception mandate. At the heart of the issue was whether religious organizations other than churches were exempt from participating in a program that would violate the consciences of their members. The Little Sisters of the Poor, a Catholic religious order that runs homes for the elderly, could not abide by the mandate because contraception is forbidden by Roman Catholic teaching. In November 2015, the Supreme Court consolidated the Little Sisters of the Poor case with six similar suits (including evangelical challenges to the Affordable Care Act by Geneva College, East Texas Baptist University, and Southern Nazarene University) under the case *Zubik v. Burwell*. The following March, the court issued a *per curiam* decision that sent the case back to the appellate courts. For the moment these religious institutions are exempt, but the fight continues. During the 2016 presidential election campaign, the Little Sisters of the Poor gained national attention when candidates such as Ted Cruz and Marco Rubio used the order's legal problems to convince evangelical voters that their religious liberties were also under attack.

Abortion and health care were not the only concerns that evangelicals had about the Obama presidency. Same-sex marriage was also a major battlefield in the ongoing culture wars. In 1996, the House of Representatives and the Senate passed the Defense of Marriage Act. The act defined marriage as "a legal union between one man and one woman as husband and wife" and declared that the word "spouse" refers "only to a person of the opposite sex who is a husband or a wife." In addition to defining the meaning of marriage for federal purposes, the Defense of Marriage Act gave states the right to deny the marriage of same-sex couples. Bill Clinton signed the bill into law.[16]

When he ran for president in 2008, Barack Obama supported same-sex unions, but he defended *marriage* as a union uniquely between a man and a woman. During the first two years of his first term in office, he supported the Defense of Marriage Act, but in February 2011 he changed his position and instructed the attorney general, Eric Holder, to stop defending it in court. In a May 2012 interview with Robin Roberts of ABC News, Obama announced that he had gone through an "evolution" on the issue of gay marriage to the point that he was now willing to affirm that "same-sex couples should be able to get married."[17] In 2013, the Supreme Court, in *United States v. Windsor*, declared the Defense of Marriage Act unconstitutional, and the Obama administration began extending federal rights and benefits to same-sex couples. By 2015, when the court ruled in *Obergefell v. Hodges* that the United States government must recognize same-sex marriages, the practice was already legal in thirty-six states and Washington, DC. On the evening of the decision, Obama showed his appreciation by lighting up the White House in rainbow colors.

Evangelical leaders responded quickly to the decision. The National Association of Evangelicals issued a statement proclaiming that "nothing in the Supreme Court's *Obergefell v. Hodges* opinion changes the truth about marriage. What has changed is the legal definition of marriage, which is now at variance with orthodox biblical faith as it has been affirmed across centuries and as it is embraced today by nearly two billion Christians in every nation on earth." Jim Daly, the president of Focus on the Family, proclaimed that "no court can change the eternal truth that marriage is, and always has been, between a man and a woman." He urged Focus on the Family supporters to avoid "combative and caustic" language and "remain faithful . . . to what Christ has called us to and redeemed us for." Russell Moore, the president of the Ethics and Religious Liberty Commission of the Southern Baptist Convention, saw the high court's decision as an opportunity for the church to bear witness to its historical teaching on marriage. He urged his fellow Southern Baptists to avoid fear and to build stable heterosexual marriages as they are commanded to do by God. Franklin Graham turned to his Facebook page to condemn the decision and asked people to pray that God would "spare America from his judgment." Samuel Rodriguez, the president of the National Hispanic Christian Leadership Conference, affirmed the court's "recognition to uphold proper protection of religious organizations and persons, under the First Amendment rights, as they seek to teach . . . the biblical definition of marriage as a sacred union between one man and one woman."[18]

Other responses on the right were less calm. Rod Dreher, an Eastern Orthodox Christian with a large evangelical following, offered a more apocalyptic response to the legalization of same-sex marriage. In an article on *Time* magazine's website that was published on the day of the Supreme Court decision, Dreher echoed what many ordinary evangelicals were feeling: "We are living in a culturally post-Christian nation," he wrote, warning that "LGBT activists and their fellow travelers really will be coming after social conservatives." The time has come, Dreher argued, when believers in traditional marriages "are going to have to live as exiles in our own country." It was time for Christians to "change the way we practice our faith and teach it to our children, to build resilient communities." He described this new approach as the "Benedict Option," a reference to a Christian saint who spurred the rise of monasticism.[19]

In the end, evangelical opponents of *Obergefell v. Hodges* realized that it would be very difficult to turn back the clock on same-sex marriage. The die had been cast. As a result, they took an approach to gay marriage that was slightly different from their long-standing response to *Roe v. Wade*. Since the Supreme Court made abortion legal in 1973, evangelicals have worked tirelessly to overturn the decision by trying to stack the court with pro-life justices. The response to *Obergefell v. Hodges* still required conservative justices, but the strategy focused less on overturning the Supreme Court's decision and more on the preservation of religious freedom. As sociologist Robert P. Jones has noted, conservative evangelicals became less concerned with religious liberty as "negative liberty protecting interference with freedom of worship" and more as an assertion "that individuals should be able to carry religious objections from their private life into their public roles as service providers, business owners, and even elected officials." Jones adds: "Seen in this light, the new religious liberty battles are best understood as a rearguard insurgency that is specifically designed to secure in isolated strongholds what White Christian America has lost on the field."[20] When a Kentucky county clerk named Kim Davis refused to issue a marriage license to a gay couple because it would, she said, violate her conscience, she became a focus of the national controversy centered on this new approach to religious liberty.

Having found its footing on the progressive side of the same-sex marriage issue, the Obama administration became relentless in its advocacy of social policies that not only made traditional evangelicals cringe but also infused them with a sense of righteous anger. The Obama White House issued executive orders and other decrees requiring, for example, Christian bakers to bake wedding cakes for same-sex couples. He decreed that public schools must allow transgender students to use bathrooms that coincided with the gender with which they identified.

The Obama White House's commitment to same-sex marriage also had implications for Christian colleges. D. Michael Lindsay, the president of Gordon College, a private evangelical liberal arts college in Wenham, Massachusetts, learned this the hard way. Because of its evangelical convictions, Gordon College does not hire homosexuals to be faculty members, nor does it endorse gay marriage. When Lindsay signed a letter written by evangelical leaders requesting a religious exemption to a proposed executive order preventing federal contractors from discriminating in hiring based on sexual orientation, he faced serious backlash. The mayor of neighboring Salem ended Gordon's contract to manage a historical building in the town; a local school district refused to accept student teachers from the college; and the New England Association of Schools and Colleges considered stripping Gordon of its accreditation.[21]

Jones notes that "no issue captures White Christian America's loss of cultural power better than the rapid rise in public support for same-sex marriage."[22] For more than two millennia, the belief that marriage is a union between a man and a woman served as a bedrock of Western civilization. As late as 1996, the United States, through the Defense of Marriage Act, had remained true to this definition of marriage. The changes to the government's position on marriage came quickly—too quickly for many Americans. When LGBT activists claimed that Obama was on the "right side of history" in his support of gay marriage, the message to evangelicals was clear: they were on the wrong side.

It is difficult to overestimate the speed with which this turnabout happened when we seek to understand how a large number of evangelicals voted in 2016. As the presidential election cycle began, evangelicals felt marginalized and even threatened by the social progressivism they witnessed under Obama's administration. The traditional institutions they deemed essential to a healthy society—the society that was at the core of their childhood and upbringing—was crumbling around them, and they were terrified. The country was not getting better; it was getting worse.[23] It was evangelicals' turn to call for "change." And there were plenty of presidential candidates ready to exploit their fears in exchange for political gain.

GOP Fear-Mongers

Fears of rapid moral decline would seem like unpromising territory for Donald Trump to work, but he was a quick learner. He also had a lot of help. To learn how to appeal to evangelicals, all he had to do was watch his GOP primary opponents to see how it was done—and then use his political savvy to do it better.

One of those opponents, Mike Huckabee, was a known commodity among conservative evangelicals. During the first four months of 2015 he criticized Barack and Michelle Obama for allowing their daughters to listen to Beyoncé, reaffirmed his opposition to same-sex marriage, condemned "trashy"

New York women for swearing too much, claimed ISIL was more of a threat to Americans than the "sunburn" they get from climate change, and declared war against a "secular theocracy." When, on May 5, he announced he was running for president, he held a small and early lead among white evangelical voters. Huckabee would quickly fade from view as the field grew larger during that summer and then began to narrow in the first weeks of 2016, but the issues he raised resonated with evangelicals who were fed up with the Obama administration.

When Trump entered the race on June 16, 2015, Ben Carson, who had declared his candidacy two days before Huckabee did, had taken the lead among white evangelicals. But the popular inspirational writer was unable to withstand the summer of Trump, especially when the reality-television star came out of the gate with strong language about defending traditional marriage (ten days before the *Obergefell v. Hodges* decision), building a border wall to keep Mexican "rapists" and "criminals" out of the country, ending Obamacare, and bringing back American jobs. Trump also stood up to the "liberal media," an institution that evangelicals believed presented them and their views in a bad light. His support among evangelicals seemed to rise with every controversial statement he made. When during the first GOP debate Fox News moderator Megyn Kelly asked him to explain why he had called women "fat pigs, dogs, and slobs," Trump refused to apologize, using the question as an opportunity to attack political correctness. The following day, when describing what he deemed to be Kelly's unfair questions, he said she had "blood coming out of her eyes" and "blood coming out of her . . . wherever." Following the debate, Franklin Graham published a positive assessment of Trump's performance on his Facebook page: "He's shaking up the Republican Party and the political process overall, and it needs shaking up!" Graham did not mention Trump's remarks about Kelly's menstrual cycle.[24]

By the end of June, Trump had a double-digit lead among potential evangelical voters that he would maintain for most of the summer. His only slump among evangelicals came in September and October, when Carson enjoyed a surge in the polls. Carson, sensing that his command of the evangelical vote was slipping, mounted a direct assault on Donald Trump's faith and a strong affirmation of his own Christian beliefs. When a reporter at a rally in Anaheim, California, asked Carson how he was different from Trump, he responded: "Probably the biggest thing—I've realized where my success has come from and I don't in any way deny my faith in God." He followed this statement with a paraphrase of Proverbs 22:4: "By humility and the fear of the Lord are riches, honor, and life."[25] During this period Carson also made public statements that played to white evangelical interests. He said that the teachings of Islam disqualified Muslims from serving as president of the United States; he opposed the Obama policy of welcoming Syrian refugees; he defended the right to fly a Confederate flag on private property; he compared political correctness to what happened in Hitler's Germany; and he argued that the Holocaust could have been prevented if German Jews had been armed. Carson knew which chords to strike: Muslims, terror, race, and guns. For the first time since entering the race, Trump was running second among evangelicals.

It would not last long. By November 2015, Trump was on the offensive. He took Carson down a notch among evangelical voters by raising doubts about whether the Seventh-day Adventist Church, to which Carson belongs, was a truly Christian denomination. At a campaign rally in Jacksonville, Florida, Trump announced: "I'm Presbyterian, boy, that's down the middle of the road, folks, in all fairness. I mean, Seventh-day Adventist, I don't know about. I just don't know about." Several weeks later, Trump questioned the legitimacy of certain aspects of Carson's life story, including a claim that his belt buckle once saved him from a knife-wielding gang member. But this was only the beginning of Carson's demise. When terrorism filled the headlines, it was Trump, not Carson, who did a better job of playing the strongman. On November 13, 2015, ISIL claimed responsibility for coordinated terrorist attacks on Paris that resulted in 130 deaths. On December 2, jihadist-inspired terrorists killed fourteen people in a San Bernardino, California, health center. The day following the San Bernardino shootings Trump was on the air at Fox News proposing a strategy to kill the families of terrorists and criticizing Barack Obama for never using the phrase "radical Islamic terrorist," adding, "There's something going on with him that we don't know about." In other interviews, he called for the closing of mosques and the "total and complete shutdown" of Muslims entering the United States.[26] In December, Trump and others continued to question Carson's life story, as told in his memoir *Gifted Hands*. It didn't help that the retired neurosurgeon also made several misstatements about US foreign policy when responding to questions about Islamic terrorism.[27] By the end of the year Trump had recaptured the lead among evangelical voters, and he would not lose it again.

Trump never had a majority of evangelical GOP primary voters, but his plurality was enough. By January, only Rubio and Cruz had a legitimate chance of overcoming his lead among their fellow religionists. Rubio assembled a "religious liberty advisory board" that included Rick Warren, Samuel Rodriguez, and evangelical academics Vincent Bacote, Wayne

Grudem, and Thomas Kidd. The advisory board was the brain-child of Eric Teetsel, the campaign's director of faith outreach. Teetsel's choices spoke volumes about the kind of evangelicals Rubio wanted to reach. Bacote, a Wheaton College theology professor, had just written a book on evangelical political engagement and was a strong advocate for the role of Christianity in cultural renewal. Baylor University historian Kidd, a prolific writer on matters related to religious freedom and the American founding, published scholarly books respected by liberals and conservatives alike. Grudem, a conservative evangelical theologian, was very popular among young Calvinists for his "complementarian" view of marriage.

The Rubio advisory committee suggested that the Florida senator was trying to win the more educated and middle-of-the-road segment of white evangelicals, the people who send their children to Wheaton College or who attended churches with pastors trained at schools such as Trinity Evangelical Divinity School or Southern Baptist Theological Seminary. On the eve of the Iowa primary, Rubio appeared in a television ad that looked and sounded more like an evangelistic sermon than a political appeal. He sat in front of a simple black screen and made multiple references to his belief in the "free gift of salvation offered to us by Jesus Christ" and the need to "store up treasures in heaven." The ad said nothing about his policies.[28]

Trump, on the other hand, was appealing to a different kind of evangelical voter. His business success and wealth made him attractive to those Christians sympathetic to the gospel of prosperity, or the "health and wealth gospel" movement. Some of the powerful leaders of the Independent Network Charismatic (INC) Movement, an oft-overlooked segment of American evangelicalism, prophesied a Trump victory. In September 2015, when Trump met with nearly three dozen evangelical leaders at Trump Tower, the room was filled with Pentecostal, prosperity gospel, and INC leaders, such as Gloria and Kenneth Copeland, Jan Crouch, Paula White, and Mark Burns. By January 2016, Trump had also secured endorsements from Robert Jeffress, the pastor of the First Baptist Church of Dallas, and Jerry Falwell Jr., president of Liberty University, the largest Christian university in the world. Neither of the latter two evangelical leaders had associated themselves with the prosperity movement, but they were both entrepreneurial Christians who had built large and successful evangelical institutions.[29]

Ted Cruz's grassroots campaign among evangelicals led to his eventual victory in the Iowa caucuses on February 1. Endorsements rolled in from James Dobson, the founder of Focus on the Family ministries and one of the architects of the Christian Right's "family values" campaign, and Tony Perkins, the president of the conservative Family Research Council. Cruz's endorsers also included Ben Sasse, the popular evangelical senator from Nebraska; Michael Tait, the lead singer of the popular Christian contemporary music band Newsboys; radio commentator Glenn Beck; and conservative Christian activist and former GOP presidential candidate Gary Bauer.

Ted Cruz turned fear-mongering into an art form. The Cruz campaign mirrored the old days of the Moral Majority, the organization that Jerry Falwell founded nearly forty years earlier to reclaim America for Christ. Anyone who attended one of Cruz's rallies or watched him on television came away from the experience with a sense that he and his followers were on God's side and that everyone else was working with the forces of evil to destroy America. David Brooks described his speeches as "pagan brutalism" and characterized his campaign as laying "down an atmosphere of apocalyptic fear" in which America is "heading off the cliff to oblivion." When a religion professor from Keene State University encountered Cruz in a New Hampshire diner, the candidate referred to Ephesians 6, where the apostle Paul says, "Put on the whole armor of God, that you may be able to stand against the schemes of the devil." Cruz added: "This nation is under attack, and it's only going to get worse." Glenn Beck illustrated the political fear-mongering of the Cruz campaign when he said before the Indiana primary that, if Cruz were to lose, "you will lose freedom for all mankind. I'm convinced of it. This is the moment. Don't be on the sideline."[30]

More than any other candidate, Cruz talked about the need to "reclaim" or "restore" America. For many white conservative evangelicals, this was code for returning the United States to its supposedly Judeo-Christian roots. Cruz wanted Americans to believe that the country had fallen away from its spiritual founding and that he, with God's help, was the man who could bring it back.

Those who followed Cruz's campaign closely knew that he regularly referred to the important role that his father, traveling evangelist Rafael Cruz, had played in his life. During a 2012 sermon at New Beginnings Church in Bedford, Texas, Rafael Cruz described his son's campaign for a Senate seat as a direct fulfillment of biblical prophecy. The elder Cruz told the congregation that God would anoint Christian "kings" to preside over an "end-time transfer of wealth" from the wicked to the righteous. After this sermon, Larry Huch, the pastor of New Beginnings, claimed that Cruz's recent election to the US Senate was a sign that he was one of those kings. According to his father and Huch, Ted Cruz was anointed by God to help Christians in their effort to "go to the marketplace and occupy

the land . . . and take dominion" over it. This "end-time transfer of wealth" would relieve Christians of all financial woes,
allowing true believers to ascend to a position of political and
cultural power so that they could build a Christian civilization.
When this Christian nation would be set in place (or back in
place), Jesus would return.

When Cruz talked about the free exercise clause of the
First Amendment—and he did so frequently—he almost always discussed it in the context of persecution against Christians. In a November speech at an Assemblies of God church
in Orlando, Florida, Cruz pulled no punches. "We have a situation in this country," he told his largely evangelical audience,
"America's in crisis. We're bankrupting our kids and grand-
kids. Our constitutional rights are under assault each and every day." He stoked fears of national security seasoned with
attacks on the liberal media:

> The media doesn't like to talk about the problems from
> illegal immigration, they don't like to talk about the
> crime as people cross the borders and commit crimes
> and we don't know who's coming in. The media doesn't
> like to talk about the national security threats, as you
> have countries that are serious threats with their na-
> tionals crossing the southern border that we don't
> know who they are. We don't know where they're
> coming from, whether it is ISIS or Ebola. Our ability
> to detect who's coming into this country and threat-
> ening the people of America is negligible as long as
> the federal government is not securing the borders.

Cruz went on and on, calling attention to murderers and
sexual predators crossing illegally into the United States

under the Obama administration's pervasive "lawlessness." Anyone who took his speech to heart probably left Faith Assembly Church of God in Orlando that night afraid that the end was near.[31]

During a January 2016 appearance at an Iowa Christian bookstore, Cruz told the audience, "If we come together as 'we the people,' then we will restore, we will bring back, that last best hope for mankind, that shining city on a hill that is the United States of America." The statement was a jumbled mix of references to the United States Constitution, the Sermon on the Mount, John Winthrop's famous phrase describing the Christian utopian society he hoped to build in seventeenth-century Massachusetts Bay, and Ronald Reagan's adoption of that phrase in the 1980s to describe American greatness. Many evangelicals love this blending of God and country, and Cruz knew it.[32]

Already hitting his stride with his base, Cruz gained a new talking point in mid-February, with Super Tuesday only a couple of weeks away. When conservative Supreme Court justice Antonin Scalia died suddenly on a quail hunting trip in Texas, and it became clear that the Republican-controlled Senate would not provide a hearing for Merrick Garland, Barack Obama's appointee to replace Scalia, the presidential election of 2016 became a referendum on the future of the high court. Scalia was a champion of the social values that conservative evangelicals hold dear, and it was now clear that the newly elected president of the United States would appoint his successor.

Cruz seized the day. Two days after Scalia died and five days before the 2016 South Carolina primary, Cruz released a political ad in the hopes of capitalizing on evangelical fears about the justice's replacement. With a picture of the Supreme

Court building as a backdrop, the narrator said, "Life, marriage, religious liberty, the Second Amendment. We're just one Supreme Court justice away from losing them all." In an interview with NBC's *Meet the Press*, Cruz said that a vote for Hillary Clinton, Bernie Sanders, or Donald Trump could lead American citizens to lose some of their rights. "We are one justice away from the Second Amendment being written out of the constitution altogether," he said. "And if you vote for Donald Trump in this next election, you are voting for undermining our Second Amendment right to keep and bear arms." Cruz pushed this appeal to evangelical fear even harder at a Republican Women's Club meeting in Greenville, South Carolina. He told these Republican voters that the United States was "one justice away" from "the Supreme Court mandating unlimited abortion on demand," and for good measure he added that it was only a matter of time before the federal government started using chisels to "remove the crosses and the Stars of David from the tombstones of our fallen soldiers."[33]

The Strongman

Cruz and the rest of the evangelical GOP contenders understood evangelical fear and could play to it in their primary campaign much more effectively than Donald Trump could. Between the summer of 2015 and the start of the primary season in early 2016, they were able to diagnose the crisis that the United States was facing in a way that brought great anxiety and concern to American evangelicals. But their strategy backfired: with their fears now stirred to a fever pitch, not enough evangelicals believed that Cruz, Rubio, or Carson could protect them from the progressive social forces wreaking havoc on their Christian nation. The evangelical candidates stoked fears of a world they seemed unfit to tame. Desperate times called for a strongman, and if a strongman was needed, only Donald Trump would fit the bill. Robert Jeffress told the *Dallas Observer* in April 2016:

> When I'm looking for a leader who's gonna sit across the negotiating table from a nuclear Iran, or who's gonna be intent on destroying ISIS, I couldn't care less about that leader's temperament or his tone or his vocabulary. Frankly, I want the meanest, toughest son of a gun I can find. And I think that's the feeling of a lot of evangelicals. They don't want a Casper Milquetoast as the leader of the free world.[34]

In a September 2016 lecture at Messiah College, conservative *New York Times* columnist Ross Douthat told a packed audience that in a post-Christian age, evangelicals might find themselves relying more heavily on political strongmen to shield them from rushing secularization. In one of the more stinging lines of the talk, Douthat suggested that evangelicals seem to need Trump, a man with no real Christian conviction to speak of, to protect them in the same way that Syrians needed the brutal dictator Bashar al-Assad to protect them against the threat of ISIL.

Trump was no novice when it came to fear-mongering, and despite his apparent lack of evangelical credentials, he found his way into the mainstream of evangelical anxieties quickly. Already his December 2015 call to ban all Muslim immigration to the United States had resonated with many conservative evangelicals. In July 2017, the Pew Research Center reported that 72 percent of white evangelicals believed that

Islam and democracy were in conflict, prompting *Christianity Today*, the flagship magazine of anti-Trump white evangelicalism, to run an article entitled "Most White Evangelicals Don't Believe Muslims Belong in America."[35] Shortly before the Iowa primary, Trump spoke at the Liberty University convocation and told students and others in attendance that he was going to "protect Christianity" and would never allow American Christians to experience the same fate as Christians in Syria, where ISIS was "chopping off heads." Whenever Trump promised to dismantle the presidential legacy of Barack Obama (and several commentators and journalists have suggested that Trump is "obsessed" with Obama), evangelicals concluded that he meant abortion, the Affordable Care Act, same-sex marriage, religious liberty, and a host of other progressive reforms.[36]

Here, then, was someone who sounded like a *real* strongman, whose tough talk made him seem to many to be strong enough to stand up to the terrors of the age. He quickly found the perfect approach. Despite his wealth and power, Trump presented himself as an embattled outsider—as many evangelicals now saw themselves—who always rose triumphant over the myriad forces trying to bring him down. He was a "winner," and he managed to convince American evangelicals that he could score a culture-war victory on their behalf. He would shelter them from Mexican strangers threatening white evangelical America. He would protect them from Muslims prepared to kill them and their families. He would defend them from political correctness, propagated by the liberal media, which discriminated against them. He would deliver the Supreme Court.[37]

By the end of May 2016, Donald Trump had enough delegates to clinch the Republican Party's nomination for president. Nearly half of GOP evangelicals supported him in that spring's primaries. Furthermore, over the course of the next few months, Trump's campaign grew stronger among evangelical voters when the Democratic Party nominated Hillary Clinton to oppose him in the general election. The evangelical politics of fear now had its last necessary threat officially in place.

CHAPTER 2

THE PLAYBOOK

> Fear not, little flock, for it is your Father's good pleasure to give you the kingdom.
>
> — Luke 12:32

The Bible teaches that Christians are to fear God—and only God. All other forms of fear reflect a lack of faith, a failure to place one's trust completely in a providential God who has promised to work all things out for good for those who love him (Rom. 8:28). God's sovereign control over our lives and the world he created constitutes what theologian Scott Bader-Saye has called "a coherent story, a drama in which God and humankind, together, drive the story toward its proper conclusion."[1] The "proper conclusion" to the Christian story—the direction in which history is ultimately moving—is the return of Jesus Christ amid the new heaven and the new earth. But in a world filled with distractions, it is easy to let this glorious hope become smothered by fear.

God never promised Christians safety. No matter what

Joel Osteen and the other purveyors of the "prosperity gospel" tell us, God does not assure us a comfortable middle-class life. Safety and security too often draw our attention away from the things that matter most. When I was in divinity school, I had a friend named Tim. He was a relatively new Christian, and his recent conversion had led him to take seriously God's call to abandon the things that serve as our greatest sources of anxiety—wealth, status, possessions. Tim knew that if an eternal home awaited him one day, then he had nothing to fear. He endeavored to live, in accordance with Peter's first epistle, as an "alien and stranger" in this world. Tim knew that something better awaited; but, in the meantime, he aimed to follow his Savior in a spirit of hope and to do what he could to advance God's kingdom. These deeply held beliefs permeated every aspect of Tim's life, including the way he signed his personal correspondence. Rather than following proper etiquette by ending his letters with phrases such as "Sincerely Yours," "Yours Truly," or "Best Wishes," Tim concluded his epistles to fellow Christians with this phrase: "May you suffer and die for Christ." I must admit that I was a bit startled when I went to my mailbox one afternoon and found my first note from Tim signed, "May you suffer and die for Christ, Tim." But the more I thought about it, the more I realized that my friend took seriously the words of Dietrich Bonhoeffer: "When Christ calls a man, he bids him come and die."

Even the most cursory reading of the Old and New Testament reveals that, ultimately, Christians have nothing to fear. Scripture reminds us that we already have a strong protector in times of need. Moses told the Israelites to "fear not, stand firm, and see the salvation of the Lord, which he will work for you today." Amid Job's suffering, God told him: "At destruction and famine you shall laugh, and shall not fear the beasts of the earth." We are all familiar with Psalm 23: "Even though I walk through the valley of the shadow of death, I will fear no evil, for you are with me; your rod and your staff, they comfort me." Later the psalmist writes: "You will not fear that terror of the night, nor the arrow that flies by day." In 1 John we read that there is "no fear in love, but perfect love casts out fear." In the Gospel of Luke, Jesus says, "Fear not, little flock, for it is your Father's good pleasure to give you the kingdom." The author of Hebrews proclaims this: "So we can confidently say, 'The Lord is my helper, I will not fear; what can man do to me?'" American evangelicals certainly intend to take the Bible seriously. What might these passages mean for American evangelicals who have turned to political strongmen to save them from the anxieties of this world?

Fear is a natural human response in times of trouble or difficulty; the fear we have is evidence that we live in a broken world. We should expect to be afraid. But my pastor reminded us about trust on a recent Sunday morning:

> We are operating more out of fear than out of trust in God. We are afraid, and there is no good result from engaging the world from a place of fear. . . . It causes us to trust in the wrong people and the wrong things to protect us. I see it in us. We are turning to the wrong saviors. We think our salvation lies somewhere where it does not. [We are] grasping at power in our current cultural atmosphere and trying to maintain influence. By the way, that's not the way to get influence—to continue grasping at it desperately. . . . The person who is afraid long enough will always turn angry. Fear never leads to peace. Fear never leads to joy. It always leads to anger, usually anger at those who are not like you.[2]

The kind of spiritual courage necessary to overcome fear is not easy. For Christians, it can only be cultivated through the spiritual disciplines that draw us closer to God and others. Fear is an ever-present reality on this side of eternity, but when we encounter it, we should feel it leading us toward a deeper reliance on God and his grace. The hymnist John Newton put it best: "'Twas grace that taught my heart to fear, and grace my fears relieved."

Enemies Without, Enemies Within

Fear often rears its ugly head in times of great social and cultural change. In the 1950s, sociologist Will Herberg said that the moral core of American culture was built on the beliefs of the Protestant, Catholic, and Jew.[3] Evangelicals, mainline Protestants, Roman Catholics, and Jews had serious theological differences, but they could all agree that the United States was morally superior to the atheistic communism of the Soviet Union because it was built on a Judeo-Christian way of life. When Martin Luther King Jr. and his fellow participants in the civil rights movement spoke out courageously against segregation, lynching, and Jim Crow laws, they always appealed to a shared Judeo-Christian heritage and regularly used the phrase "Christian nation" to describe their country.[4] As recently as the late 1970s, President Jimmy Carter turned to religious faith as a source of the common good that he insisted must hold us together as a nation in an age of narcissism.

But by the 1980s, Americans were living through what historian Daniel Rodgers calls "the age of fracture." The Reagan era, for all its celebration of Judeo-Christian values, friendliness toward evangelicals, and "God and country" language, was marked by a continuing shift away from a collective sense of national unity and toward an American identity defined by membership in particular groups. "Identity politics" stemming from the cultural shifts of the 1960s emphasized the distinctiveness and needs of particular groups in American society at the expense of the nationalism that King and others drew on so heavily during the early civil rights movement. Ideological battles over the teaching of American history and an "originalist" reading of the Constitution further divided the nation, creating what sociologist James Davison Hunter described as the "culture wars."[5]

Evangelicals saw the fractures as a threat to the nation's moral core. After they awoke to these changes, they organized politically and sought to put the American Humpty Dumpty back together again, with their own religious narrative at the core of the national-origin story. Newly awakened to their political power, feeling spurned by the progressive policies of Jimmy Carter, and deeply afraid of the direction the national culture seemed to be going in, they abandoned their earlier reluctance to become involved in politics and mobilized to fight back via politics. The political attempts to mend these fractures are still with us today. Evangelicals voted for Trump because they have been conditioned to a way of thinking about political engagement that emerged in the 1970s and 1980s as a direct response to these cultural changes.

A Perfect Storm

In the decade and a half following World War II, the United States experienced nothing short of a religious revival. President Dwight D. Eisenhower proclaimed: "Without God there could be no American form of government, nor an American way of life." During that fifteen years (1945–1960), the US population grew by 19 percent, but church attendance grew by 30 percent. By 1960, 69 percent of Americans belonged to a church or synagogue. In 1953, when Eisenhower signed a statement drafted by the National Association of Evangelicals proclaiming that "the United States of America had been founded on the principle of the Holy Bible," very few people thought twice about it. Shortly thereafter, Congress approved an act to add the words "under God" to the Pledge of Allegiance, and to place the words "In God We Trust" on US coins and paper currency. The godly nation seemed to be thriving. Christianity provided meaning to the lives of American soldiers as they returned home from war, started families, and moved to the suburbs. As the cold war emerged and threatened, God seemed to be on the side of the United States.[6]

But as the American revival flourished, the judicial branch of the federal government was unimpressed. Historian Daniel K. Williams says that, "while politicians in the 1950s had bolstered American civil religion by equating religious faith with patriotism, the Supreme Court had been moving in the opposite direction and had, since the late 1940s, attempted to shore up the wall between church and state."[7] In 1947, the Supreme Court heard the case of *Everson v. Board of Education*. The plaintiff, Arch R. Everson, was a member of a New Jersey chapter of the nativist, anti-Catholic Junior Order of United American Mechanics. One of the order's agenda priorities was to stop a New Jersey law allowing taxpayer money to be used for the busing of children to Catholic schools. Everson and his lawyers argued that the New Jersey busing law was a violation of the "absolute separation of church and state" as affirmed in the First Amendment.[8]

For many conservative evangelicals today, the defenders of the "separation of church and state" represent the enemy. Conservatives demonize these constitutional defenders as people who want to keep religion out of public life, and thus as secular humanists who are undermining the Christian values that supposedly built this nation. Yet, for most of American history, Protestants—including evangelical Protestants—have supported the idea of separation of church and state. This principle, which Protestants believed best reflected the idea behind the disestablishment clause of the First Amendment to the US Constitution, provided a defense not only against government incursions into their churches but also against long-standing Catholic threats to a Protestant nation. In his 1895 encyclical *Longinqua,* or "On Catholicism in the United States," Pope Leo XIII called for Catholics to contribute to American "greatness" by advancing Catholic learning, forming labor unions, pursuing vocations in journalism, and engaging in evangelism. Between 1945 and 1960, the Catholic population in the United States grew by 90 percent. Bishops, priests, women religious, and laypersons built seminaries, hospitals, relief agencies, parochial schools, and colleges.[9]

Protestants worried about this Catholic invasion. The mainline Protestant magazine *Christian Century* represented all concerned Protestants, including evangelicals, when it published a thirteen-part series in 1946 entitled "Can Protestantism Win America?" Editor Charles Clayton Morrison was afraid that Protestantism would lose its "ascendant position in the American community" to this rising Catholic threat. In their assertions that the United States needed to keep church and state "separate," white Protestants revealed that the church they most wanted to keep separate from the state was the Catholic Church.

In the end, the Supreme Court decided that New Jersey *would* be allowed to use public funds to bus students to parochial schools. Protestants were angry with the decision because it seemed to undermine the separation of church and state and failed to strike a blow to the "Catholic menace." Yet despite ruling for the Catholic schools, the Supreme Court's majority insisted that it *was* maintaining the separation of church and state. Justice Hugo Black, drawing on Thomas Jefferson's famous 1802 letter to the Baptists of Danbury, Connecticut, declared: "In the words of Jefferson, the clause against establishment of religion by law was intended to erect 'a wall of separation between church and state.'. . . That wall must be kept high and impregnable. We could not approve the slightest breach." The *Everson* decision also incorporated the religion clauses of the First Amendment into the Fourteenth Amendment, meaning that these clauses now applied to the states. What most Protestants did not realize at the time was that, thirty years later, Black's words about the "high and impregnable" wall would trigger a culture war over the proper relationship between religion, government, and public life. It was only a matter of time before the court would use Black's opinion in *Everson*, or at least the spirit of that decision, to undermine their notion of a Christian nation.[10]

In 1962, in *Engel v. Vitale*, the "wall of separation" was applied to prayer in public schools. The case revolved around a prayer composed by the New York Board of Regents that school children in the Empire State would be required to recite at the start of each school day. It read: "Almighty God, we acknowledge our dependence upon Thee, and we beg Thy blessings upon us, our parents, our teachers, and our Country." When a group of non-Christian families with children in a Long Island school district objected to the prayer, the case made its way to

the Supreme Court where, once again, Black wrote the majority decision. Black argued that government should not be in
the business of writing prayers for public-school children to
recite in class. He concluded that "when power, prestige, and
financial support of government is placed behind a particular
religious belief, the indirect coercive pressure upon religious
minorities to conform to the prevailing officially approved
religion is plain." The so-called Regents' Prayer was a clear
violation of the disestablishment clause.[11]

As historian Kevin Kruse has noted, opposition to *Engel v.
Vitale* was exacerbated by the press coverage of the decision. It
was not uncommon for major metropolitan newspapers to run
headlines such as "God Banned from the States." Billy Graham
described the decision as "another step toward secularism."
But eventually *Engel v. Vitale* was accepted by the evangelical community. Evangelical magazines such as *Christianity
Today* rejected the "least common denominator religion" that
the Regents Prayer promoted. It was the job of churches, not
the state, the editors argued, to teach children to pray. Even
Graham eventually accepted the decision.[12] Yet somehow the
Supreme Court's reasoning failed to satisfy the next generation of conservative evangelicals, who would use the case to
strengthen their grand narrative of spiritual decline in the
United States.

One year later, the Supreme Court ruled on mandatory
Bible-reading in public schools. *School District of Abington
Township v. Schempp* overturned a fourteen-year-old Pennsylvania law requiring teachers to read ten Bible verses to
their students at the start of each school day. In 1956, Ellory
Schempp, a Unitarian high school student in Abington, Pennsylvania, refused to participate in the daily Bible-reading ceremony, preferring instead to read a copy of the Koran while

remaining seated at his desk. The Supreme Court ruled that Bible-reading for devotional purposes was unconstitutional— yet another violation of the disestablishment clause in the post-*Everson* era.

The evangelical response to *Abington v. Schempp* was more negative than the response to *Engel v. Vitale* had been. It was one thing to take prayer-writing out of the hands of state entities; it was quite another to take the Bible out of schools. Evangelicals are people of the sacred book, and they saw the removal of Bible-reading in schools as a direct attack on America's Protestant character. Harold John Ockenga, the pastor of Boston's Park Street Church and the first president of Fuller Theological Seminary, said that the removal of the Bible from public schools was something he expected to happen in communist Russia, not in America. Dr. Robert A. Cook, president of the National Association of Evangelicals, said that the decision was a "sad departure from this nation's heritage under God." Bible-lovers flooded the American Bible Society in New York City with letters asking for help in overturning the decision. Neither *Abington v. Schempp* nor *Engel v. Vitale* had much public support; in August 1963, the pollster George Gallup concluded that 70 percent of Americans supported prayer and Bible-reading in public schools.

Protestants intensified their opposition to both Supreme Court decisions during the next few years. Several legislators, most prominently Illinois Republican Everett Dirksen, proposed a constitutional amendment that would allow prayer in public schools, essentially overturning *Engel v. Vitale*. The so-called Dirksen Amendment fell nine votes short in the Senate. Many Protestants believed that if they could overturn *Engel v. Vitale*, they could do the same to *Abington v. Schempp*. But it was not to be.[13]

As the Supreme Court began to dismantle some of the important rituals of Protestant political and cultural power in America, the demographic makeup of the country was also on the verge of a significant transformation. In 1965, as part of Lyndon B. Johnson's Great Society program, the United States Congress passed the Immigration and Nationality Act, also known as the Hart-Celler Act. The new law ended the immigration quotas based on national origins that had been at the center of American immigration policy since 1921. These quotas had given preference to northern and western Europeans as part of an effort to reduce the number of southern and eastern Europeans who had arrived on American shores between 1880 and 1920. The Hart-Celler Act replaced national-origins quotas with hemispheric quotas that favored immigrants from the Eastern hemisphere (170,000 per year) over the Western hemisphere (120,000 per year).[14]

We should not overlook the legacy of the Hart-Celler Act if we wish to understand the fears many white conservative evangelicals have today about strangers coming to America and undermining their Christian nation. This new immigration law brought unprecedented racial and ethnic diversity to the United States. Seven million immigrants—most of them from Mexico, the Dominican Republic, Cuba, Haiti, and other parts of Latin America and the Caribbean —came to live in the United States between 1966 and 1993. Five million more arrived from Asia and the Pacific, with the largest numbers coming from China, Korea, Vietnam, India, and the Philippines.

In one sense, these immigrants were like previous waves of newcomers to the United States. They came from poor and undeveloped parts of the world, and they adjusted to their new surroundings through close-knit patriarchal families and neighborhoods. But the things that made them unique were just the things that many white conservative evangelicals feared the most about them: they practiced non-Western religions, such as Islam (the fastest-growing religion in the United States after the passage of the Hart-Celler Act), Hinduism, and Buddhism. They were not white. But they were also often critical of the low level of morality that capitalism and individualism tended to foster in the American youth culture, though this traditionalist morality was almost never mentioned by those who did not want them as neighbors.[15]

The Hart-Celler Act was not the only issue related to race that white evangelicals had to come to grips with in the 1960s and 1970s. In general, white evangelicals throughout the country had a mixed track record regarding the racial issues facing the country during the civil rights movement. Billy Graham was famous for desegregating his evangelistic crusades, and many evangelical leaders and publications supported the *Brown v. Board of Education* decision ending segregation in public schools, just as they supported the Civil Rights Act (1964) and the Voting Rights Act (1965). But very few Northern evangelicals actually participated in the movement, and strong pockets of segregationist thought and practice continued to exist in the evangelical South. Most white evangelicals were not particularly interested in the civil rights movement; they were far more concerned about—and opposed to—the way the federal government used its power to enforce desegregation and oppose Jim Crow laws in their local communities. Historian Mark Noll has argued that race and civil rights served as an entry point for the white conservative evangelical critique of active government.[16]

The relationship between race and evangelical opposition to "big government" intervention into state and local affairs is best illustrated in the evangelical response to two Supreme Court cases. *Green v. Connally* (1972) removed tax-exempt status from private schools and colleges that discriminated against students based on race. At the center of the controversy was Bob Jones University, a school that banned interracial dating and denied admission to unmarried African Americans. In 1975, the IRS moved to revoke the tax-exempt status of the university, a case that was eventually decided in favor of the IRS in *Bob Jones v. United States*. *Green v. Connally* and *Bob Jones v. United States* also had implications for the hundreds of private Christian academies cropping up (at a rate of two per day) all over the United States. Many of these schools were in the South and had discriminatory admissions policies, which is not surprising given that many such schools were founded in the immediate aftermath of public-school integration. When President Jimmy Carter, a self-proclaimed "born-again Christian," supported the *Green v. Connally* decision, he alienated many conservative evangelicals who ran these academies. To be fair, many segregationist academies were already beginning to admit African American students in the early 1970s, but the leaders of these schools, true to their Southern heritage, wanted to deal with the issues of segregation, race, and civil rights on their own terms. They certainly did not want the federal government forcing them to desegregate.[17]

Shortly after *Green v. Connally*, yet another Supreme Court case reminded American evangelicals that the moral fabric of what was once their great Christian nation was continuing to fray. When the court declared, in *Roe v. Wade*, that certain kinds of abortion were legal in the United States, evangelicals did not have a track record of fighting to protect human life in a mother's womb. Most evangelicals thought abortion was a moral problem, and they believed that the pro-life movement was a distinctly Catholic crusade. But in the context of these other decisions that put "Christian America" on the defensive, *Roe v. Wade* awakened evangelicals to the view that abortion was equivalent to legalized murder and that the federal government was now endorsing the practice. As *Christianity Today* opined in the wake of the decision, "Christians should accustom themselves to the thought that the American state no longer supports, in any meaningful sense, the laws of God, and prepare themselves spiritually for the prospect that it may one day formally repudiate them and turn against those who seek to live by them." The evangelical opposition to a woman's right to choose was also tied to its opposition to the rising feminist movement and the attempt in 1972 to pass an Equal Rights Amendment to the United States Constitution. For most evangelicals, feminism threatened their understanding of family structure in the home *and* endangered infants in the womb: they were not only to be considered children of God but also the natural gifts of traditional motherhood.[18]

Between 1947 and the election of Ronald Reagan, evangelicals witnessed a renewed emphasis on the separation of church and state, the removal of prayer and Bible-reading from public schools, the influx of immigrants from non-Western nations who practiced a variety of non-Christian religions, the intrusion of the federal government into their schools, and the court's endorsement of abortion on demand. They beheld a perfect storm capable of wiping out the Christian ideals that built their great nation. Supreme Court decisions, changes in demographics, and progressive policy shifts even under a born-again Christian president seemed difficult to beat back, but white conservative evangelicals would give it their best shot.

The Playbook of the Christian Right

As America faced long gas lines and a hostage crisis in Iran, conservative evangelicals were preparing to take back their country. The Bicentennial in 1976 offered an ideal moment to reflect on the history of the United States and offer a revisionist narrative of the American founding that placed God at the center. As we will see in chapter 5, the idea that the United States was founded as a Christian nation undergirded the political agenda of what would soon become the "Christian Right." Without such revisionism, evangelical arguments for a return of prayer and Bible-reading to public schools, their libertarian rejection of big government, and their opposition to *Roe v. Wade* would lack solid historical footing: that is, they would be just another interest group advocating for its particular point of view. But if America was founded as a Christian nation, conservative evangelicals could invoke the Founding Fathers to defend displaying the Ten Commandments in courthouses, praying at school graduation ceremonies, and even the belief that the First Amendment protections of religious freedoms applied primarily to Christians. Tim LaHaye, a popular evangelical author, declared in 1990 that the "removal of God from public life" in the years since *Everson* had led to an increase in sexual permissiveness, unwed pregnancies, and venereal disease. David Barton, a conservative evangelical activist with an interest in the American past, added a few more social ills to LaHaye's list, including a rise in violent crime, lower SAT scores, and the growth of single-family households.[19]

Many of these culture warriors found intellectual support for their agenda from Francis Schaeffer, an evangelical guru who attracted hundreds of bright young Christian minds to

L'Abri, his chalet and study center in the Swiss Alps. During the 1970s, Schaeffer became a household name among American evangelicals as he taught the sojourners who passed through L'Abri, and thousands of other thinking Christians who read his books, how to develop a "Christian world view." In a wildly popular book and film series entitled *Whatever Happened to the Human Race?* (1979), Schaeffer challenged *Roe v. Wade* on legal and philosophical grounds and defended the dignity of all human life. For Schaeffer, abortion was a sign of a larger cultural shift that placed human beings and their desires, rather than God, at the center of Western civilization. The idea that governments would allow the murder of a human life in the womb was just the latest example of a long trajectory of secularism that Schaeffer believed started during the Renaissance. Along the way, Schaeffer became interested in the writings of the Christian Reconstructionist Rousas John Rushdoony, who believed that Old Testament civil law should be binding on the people of the United States. Though Schaeffer did not agree with all of Rushdoony's ideas, he was influenced by the Reconstructionist view that the United States was founded on biblical principles.[20]

Schaeffer had a profound influence on a conservative Baptist preacher from Lynchburg, Virginia, named Jerry Falwell. Schaeffer converted Falwell to the pro-life movement, but Falwell soon proved to have a larger agenda, of which the pro-life movement would be merely a part. Falwell, the pastor of Thomas Road Baptist Church, had once been a segregationist, and during the civil rights movement he argued that ministers should not be involved in politics. Now he took Schaeffer's call to restore the United States to biblical ideals and connected it to virtually every moral issue evangelicals were concerned about since the Supreme Court had declared that the "wall of [church/state] separation" was "high and impregnable." With the help of LaHaye's book *The Battle for the Mind* (1980), Falwell became convinced that secular humanism was not only a threat to the Christian identity of the nation, but also that it was the philosophy behind intrusive federal power. The United States, he believed, was a nation built on liberty and freedom of individuals, not on the kind of centralized authority that he associated with the Soviet Union and other communist states. Falwell and like-minded conservative evangelicals had already experienced the power of the central government when the Supreme Court intruded on the affairs of their segregated academies. In fact, historian Randall Balmer contends that it was this fear of big-government interference as it related to desegregation of institutions like Bob Jones University and Falwell's own Liberty Academy that prompted the formation of the Christian Right. Paul Weyrich, one of Falwell's closest associates and one of the leading organizers of the movement, told Balmer in a 1990 interchange that the Christian Right was originally founded, not on evangelicals' opposition to abortion, but rather on opposition to the attempts by the IRS to desegregate Christian academies.[21]

Jerry Falwell gained national attention for his crusades to "clean up America." In 1976, he traveled to every state capitol in the United States, with his Lynchburg Baptist College choir in tow, to stage "I Love America" rallies. These events included patriotic songs and calls for national repentance. He also developed close relationships with conservative politicians, such as Weyrich, Robert Billings, Richard Viguerie, and Howard Phillips, many of whom were veterans of the Barry Goldwater campaign in 1964 and supported limited government and traditional values. They urged Falwell to get more involved in politics and convinced him that he could become a voice for Christian Americans who had become disgruntled with the nation's secular turn. In 1979, Falwell formed the Moral Majority, an organization designed to raise money for conservative politicians, to encourage people of faith to seize political power in the federal government, and to rid the country of pornography, abortion, and homosexuality. They fought communism, socialism, and all forms of big government—and sought to restore America to its Christian roots.

The work of Falwell and the Moral Majority had immediate results. Falwell was influential in shaping the 1980 Republican Party platform, which called for an end to the ratification process of the Equal Rights Amendment as it celebrated women as homemakers; called for a constitutional amendment "to restore protection of the right of life for unborn children"; opposed President Jimmy Carter's "unconstitutional regulatory vendetta" against "independent schools"; condemned "big government"; and supported school prayer. When Ronald Reagan defeated Carter in the 1980 presidential race, Falwell and his moral crusaders cheered. Ironically, they had rejected the first United States presidential candidate to identify himself as a "born-again Christian" and had thrown their support behind a formerly pro-choice California governor. From this point forward, conservative evangelicals would see the Republican Party as their vehicle to achieve political change.[22]

The Moral Majority—and the various manifestations of the Christian Right that would follow it—went to work on a political playbook designed to win America for their Christian agenda. As we shall see below, this playbook is still in operation today. It teaches, and has taught, Christians that the best way to reclaim America would be to elect a president and members of Congress who would pass laws granting privileges to what Schaeffer called a "Christian worldview." These elected officials would, in turn, appoint and confirm conservative Supreme Court justices who would defend religious liberty by challenging the understanding of the "separation of church and state" articulated in *Everson*, overturn *Roe v. Wade*, and defend Christian conservative values. While control of the presidency and the Congress is certainly important to the successful implementation of this playbook, the control of the Supreme Court is essential. The fracturing of the nation's Christian consensus, the Christian Right argues, took place at the hands of unelected liberal justices such as Hugo Black, whose decisions could only be overturned by new justices who had to be nominated and appointed by officials in the two elected branches of the federal government. There have been some subtle alterations to the playbook over the years: for example, in the 1990s, Pat Robertson's Christian Coalition, under the guidance of Ralph Reed, incorporated local elections; but the pursuit of politics has remained the dominant approach to winning the culture wars fostered by conservative evangelicals today. The goal is to pass Christian laws—surely the intent of the founders of this Christian nation, after all—and require everyone to live under them. Writing in 2010, James Davison Hunter noted that it is "not an exaggeration to say that the dominant public witness of the Christian churches in America since the early 1980s has been a political witness."[23]

When the playbook of the Christian Right first captured the political imagination of white conservative evangelicals and fundamentalists during the Reagan era, it exhorted evangelicals to vote not only for candidates with socially conservative policies, but also for those candidates who exemplified the highest levels of Christian character. Evangelicals, after all, have always embraced the notion that a changed heart would lead to right behavior. So it only made sense that the correct political positions on abortion, marriage, religious liberty, prayer, and Bible-reading in schools would naturally flow from the heart of a moral—preferably Christian—leader.

This commitment to the moral integrity of the office of president took center stage when the Christian Right had to deal, for the first time, with a non-Republican chief executive. Bill Clinton was a Southern Baptist, but he was pro-choice on abortion, and his wife, Hillary, seemed to reject traditional understandings of family structure by choosing full-time work in a law practice over staying home to raise her daughter. Bill Clinton shared some religious beliefs with evangelicals, but in their view he had the wrong policy positions on social issues. And when rumors began to leak out that he lacked personal character in his dealings with women, the evangelicals of the Christian Right would not let the voting public forget it. In 1994, Falwell used his television show, *The Old Time Gospel Hour*, to distribute *The Clinton Chronicles*, a documentary film on the president's supposedly immoral behavior during his years as governor of Arkansas. *The Clinton Chronicles* portrayed Clinton as a man with a "lackadaisical moral attitude" who lied repeatedly to the people of Arkansas, aided in the laundering of drug money, regularly used cocaine, and was a sex addict and serial adulterer. Though the *Washington Post* described the film as a "bizarre and unsubstantiated documentary" and *The New York Times* panned it as a "hodgepodge of sometimes crazed charges," Falwell's endorsement gave it instant credibility among conservative evangelicals.[24]

When news of Clinton's White House sexual affair with intern Monica Lewinsky became public, leaders of the Christian Right made the case that he was morally unfit to hold office. Falwell told *USA Today* that political leaders were required to "flee from all appearances of evil" and added that such standards were "immensely higher for those who invoke the name of Christ, as Bill Clinton does." In an opinion piece for the conservative magazine *Human Events,* Gary Bauer, the president of the Family Research Council, wrote that Clinton's lies about the Lewinsky affair were corrupting the morals of American young people: "These children cannot be set adrift into a culture that tells them that lying is okay, that fidelity is old-fashioned, and that character doesn't count."[25]

Perhaps the strongest critic of Clinton's moral indiscretions was James Dobson, the founder of Focus on the Family and popular Christian Right radio host. In a September 1998 letter to his supporters, Dobson made it clear not only that Clinton was unqualified for the presidency, but also that his affair with Lewinsky was a sign that the moral foundation of the nation was eroding:

> What has alarmed me throughout this episode has been the willingness of my fellow citizens to rationalize the President's behavior even after they suspected, and later knew, that he was lying. . . .
>
> How did our beloved nation find itself in this sorry mess? I believe it began not with the Lewinsky affair, but many years earlier. There was plenty of evidence during the first Presidential election that Bill Clinton had a moral problem. His affair with Gennifer Flowers, which he now admits to having lied about, was rationalized by the American people. He lied about dodging the draft, and then concocted an incredulous explanation that changed his story. He visited the Soviet Union and other hostile countries during the Vietnam War, claiming that he was only an "observer." . . . Clinton evaded questions about whether

he had used marijuana, and then finally offered his now infamous "I didn't inhale" response. There were other indications that Bill Clinton was untruthful and immoral. Why, then, did the American people ignore so many red flags? Because, and I want to give the greatest emphasis to this point, the mainstream media became enamored with Bill Clinton in 1992 and sought to convince the American people that "character doesn't matter."

As it turns out, character DOES matter. You can't run a family, let alone a country, without it. How foolish to believe that a person who lacks honesty and moral integrity is qualified to lead a nation and the world! Nevertheless, our people continue to say that the President is doing a good job even if they don't respect him personally. Those two positions are fundamentally incompatible. In the Book of James the question is posed, "Can both fresh water and salt water flow from the same spring?" (James 3:11, NIV). The answer is no.[26]

The Playbook's Ultimate Test: November 2016

For nearly four decades, conservative evangelicals have operated with the same political playbook. On one level, this playbook has failed to accomplish its goals. Abortion is still legal in the United States; Bible reading and prayer have not returned to public schools; the country is more religiously diverse than at any other point in its history; and gay marriage is now legal throughout the United States. While there have been small victories here and there, the Christian Right is not anywhere closer to winning back the culture than it was thirty years ago.

On the other hand, when it comes to indoctrinating American evangelicals in the most effective way of restoring a Christian nation and winning the culture wars, the Christian Right's playbook has been extremely successful. Despite its failure to deliver on its promises to reclaim the nation for Christ, the Christian Right has shaped the political sensibilities of millions and millions of conservative evangelicals. Alternative Christian approaches to politics have been proposed, but none of them have made any serious inroads into evangelical culture. Meanwhile, the strategy has thrust the leaders of the Religious Right into a position of tremendous influence in one of the nation's two major political parties.

But what would become of that influence in 2016? When a plurality of Republican voters made Donald Trump, rather than any of his evangelical competitors, the Republican nominee, would evangelicals turn out for him in the general election? It was a question that confounded pundits. Could *this* candidate really marshal the Religious Right to the polls?

The answer to that question lay in Trump's ability to execute the game plan in the culture-war playbook. Between May (the month he won enough delegates to wrap up the GOP nomination) and November 2016, Trump and his team worked hard at bringing more evangelicals into his fold. He chose Indiana governor Mike Pence, a politician with impeccable evangelical credentials, as his running mate.[27] He established an evangelical advisory board that included Dobson, Jerry Falwell Jr., televangelist Paula White, South Carolina megachurch pastor Mark Burns, Southern Baptist leader Richard Land, former GOP congresswoman Michelle Bachman, Dallas megachurch pastor Robert Jeffress, and longtime Christian Right activist Ralph Reed.

But Trump pulled out his most important move to win over conservative evangelicals who were still skeptical about his candidacy on May 18. On that day, the soon-to-be GOP nominee released the names of eleven judges whom he said he would consider nominating to the Supreme Court. It was a move straight out of the playbook. The list was put together with input from the Heritage Foundation, a conservative think tank known for defending traditional marriage, opposing abortion, and fighting for the right of religious institutions to avoid government interference. On July 13, 2016, the Pew Research Center released a study showing that evangelicals were rallying to Trump, and it predicted that 78 percent of white evangelical voters would support him in November.[28]

But even as Trump said all the right things to appeal to evangelical voters, these values voters still had to come to grips with an inconvenient truth: Trump appeared to be the most immoral candidate in recent memory. Trump's sins went beyond DUI convictions and the occasional recreational use of marijuana. His entire career, and his success as a television star and public figure, was built on vices incompatible with the moral teachings of Christianity. And by his own admission, he never, ever, asked for forgiveness for his sins.

At first, conservative evangelicals did not know how to respond to Trump's indiscretions. How could they support his policy proposals and ignore his serious character flaws? To do so would be to go back on much of what they had learned in church—and to undermine their own arguments that Bill Clinton's character flaws had disqualified him from fitness as president.

The only way to get around Trump's flaws was to somehow Christianize him. Paula White claimed that she had led Trump to accept Jesus Christ as his savior. Jerry Falwell Jr. said that

Trump's moral life had changed since he had become a born-again Christian. James Dobson told his followers to be patient with Trump, whom he declared to be a "baby Christian." The kind of forgiveness and understanding that was never given to Bill Clinton was now available in seemingly endless supply to Donald Trump.

But the greatest challenge to the Christian Right's ability to forgive and forget Trump's sins was still to come. On October 7, 2016, *The Washington Post* released a recording of Trump talking with Billy Bush, the host of the entertainment program *Access Hollywood*. During the lewd conversation, Trump said, "You know I'm automatically attracted to beautiful [women]—I just start kissing them. It's like a magnet. Just kiss. I don't even wait. And when you're a star, they let you do it. You can do anything. . . . Grab 'em by the pussy. You can do anything." Later Trump apologized for the remark and claimed that the conversation between him and Bush was little more than "locker-room talk." But since the *Access Hollywood* tape was released, at least twenty women have made public statements alleging that Trump had sexually assaulted or harassed them.[29]

Many conservative evangelicals condemned Trump's words on the *Access Hollywood* tape. A member of Trump's evangelical advisory council, Chicago-area megachurch pastor James MacDonald, quit.[30] But he was the only one. The majority of pro-Trump evangelical leaders either remained silent or stood behind the GOP nominee. Falwell, whose father had spoken so strongly about presidential character two decades earlier, claimed that the tape was leaked by anti-Trump members of the Republican Party. James Dobson, the great defender of the moral integrity of the office in 1998, found Trump's words to be "deplorable," but kept his endorsement of Trump because the candidate promised to support "religious liberty and the dignity of the unborn [and] Mrs. Clinton promises she will not." Ralph Reed, who in 1998 said, "Character matters, and the American people are hungry for that message," quickly dismissed Trump's words about grabbing women's genitals and redirected the conversation to corruption in the Hillary Clinton campaign. Franklin Graham responded in a similar fashion, condemning Trump's words and then turning attention to the "godless, progressive agenda of Barack Obama and Hillary Clinton."[31] The playbook was clear on this point: character simply didn't matter as much as the opportunity to seize a seat on the Supreme Court.

There is very little that Donald Trump says or does that would exemplify *Christian* character, but Trump's actions and behavior also fail to demonstrate the basic character traits that we have come to expect from *any* president of the republic, regardless of personal faith commitment. In 2010, Harvard political scientist Dennis Thompson argued that all American presidents should display a certain set of personal attributes that he called "Constitutional character." This kind of character has less to do with public or private vices and more to do with the "qualities officials should have to make the democratic process work well." These qualities include a "sensitivity to basic rights of citizenship," a "respect for due process," a "sense of responsibility," "tolerance of opposition," a "willingness to justify decisions, and "above all, the commitment to candor."[32]

Those who affiliate with the agenda of the Christian Right will be the first to say that republics rise and fall based on the virtue of the people and their leaders. One of Trump's most vocal evangelical supporters, Eric Metaxas, even wrote a book about it. In *If You Can Keep It: The Forgotten Promise of*

American Liberty, the popular author and radio host extolled the importance of moral leadership; chided Bill Clinton for devaluing the "role and dignity of the office of the president"; claimed that the character of the president has the power to influence the virtue (or lack thereof) of the American people; and urged citizens to hold their leaders to a "higher standard of behavior."[33] Metaxas is one of many pro-Trump evangelicals who claim to love the ideas of the Founding Fathers but whose adoration fades when the words of the Founders fail to affirm their political agendas. For example, they cherry-pick quotes from John Adams about the need for a moral republic, but ignore Adams when he says that the people of such a republic "have a right, indisputable, indefeasible, divine right to that most dreaded and envied kind of knowledge—I mean of the character and conduct of their rulers."[34] Evangelical supporters fail to mention the words of Publius (James Madison) in *Federalist* 57: "The aim of every political Constitution is or ought to be first to obtain for rulers, men who possess most wisdom to discern, and most virtue to pursue the common good of the society, and in the next place, to take the most effectual precautions for keeping them virtuous, whilst they continue to hold their public trust."[35] And Trump evangelical defenders never cite *Federalist* 68, the founding document in which Alexander Hamilton says: "Talents for low intrigue, and the little arts of popularity, may alone suffice to elevate a man to the first honors in a single State; but it will require other talents, and a different kind of merit, to establish him in the esteem and confidence of the whole Union, or of so considerable a portion of it as would be necessary to make him a successful candidate for the distinguished office of the president of the United States. It will not be too strong to say, that there will be a constant probability of seeing the station filled by characters pre-eminent for ability and virtue." To venerate the Founders, as so many on the Christian Right do, means coming to grips with the fact that the Founders expected the person holding the highest office in the land to be a person of character.[36] The Christian Right at least spoke the language of the Founders when they questioned Bill Clinton's fitness for office in 1998.

Evangelicals' relationship to Clinton, and to Trump, cannot be understood without mentioning the long and contentious relationship between the right and Hillary Clinton. It is impossible to understand why 81 percent of white American evangelicals turned to Donald Trump in November 2016 without grasping their strong antipathy toward Hillary Clinton. The history of that antipathy is long, reaching back at least to Bill Clinton's first campaign, when Hillary defended working in her law practice during her husband's governorship by saying, "You know, I suppose I could have stayed home and baked cookies and had teas, but what I decided to do was to fulfill my profession, which I entered before my husband was in public life." To many who embraced the importance of traditional family roles, this seemed like a disparaging attack on their values. Then, when revelations of her husband's marital infidelities surfaced, conservatives who challenged his character saw only defensiveness—and maybe something of a double standard—in Hillary's response. She seemed willing to overlook her husband's shortcomings, but she was ready to attack her husband's accusers to advance a political agenda. In a *Today Show* interview in 1998, following the Lewinsky affair, she said that the impeachment allegations against her husband were little more than a "vast right-wing conspiracy." Ironically, evangelicals' hatred of Hillary Clinton only prepared them to do exactly what she had done (defend their own political warrior against his accusers to advance their political agenda) when Hillary, long remembered as an enemy of their values, emerged as the Democratic candidate for president.

Many of these values voters had been so deeply influenced by the political playbook of the Christian Right that they were incapable of seeing Hillary Clinton, a devout mainline Methodist, as anything but the enemy. Fear of a Clinton victory blinded them to the fact that, not only did she have far more experience than Trump did, she also championed a position on paid leave that would have strengthened families, had a humane immigration policy, and defended the rights of women, children, the poor, and people of color. Many Christians see plenty of biblical themes at work in her positions, but these are not the themes long championed by the Religious Right. History—and the playbook—held: she was the enemy to be defeated.

Clinton, of course, was a deeply flawed candidate. She lied about using a private email server in her role as secretary of state. Whether or not she was responsible for the death of four Americans during a September 2012 terrorist raid on the US consulate in Benghazi, most Republican voters believed she was. Her use of the phrase "basket of deplorables" to describe Donald Trump supporters only added fuel to the sense that people with traditional values were simply being written off by Clinton and her elite allies in Washington. And she didn't help matters by making virtually no effort to court evangelical voters, a strategy that Ronald Sider, veteran of the evangelical left, called "dumbfounding and incredibly stupid."[37]

Though Clinton would never have come close to winning the evangelical vote, her tone-deafness on matters of deep importance to evangelicals may have been the final nail in the coffin of her campaign. In 2015, when a conservative pro-life group published videos showing Planned Parenthood employees discussing the purchase of the body parts and the fetal tissue of aborted fetuses, Clinton said, "I have seen the pictures [from the videos] and obviously find them disturbing."[38] Such a response could have helped her reach evangelicals on the campaign trail, but by 2016 she showed little ambivalence about abortion, or any understanding that it might pose legitimate concerns or raise larger ethical questions. During the third presidential debate, she defended a traditional pro-choice position and seemed to dodge Fox News host Chris Wallace's question about her support for late-term abortions. There seemed to be no room in her campaign for those evangelicals who didn't want to support Trump but needed to see that she could at least compromise on abortion.

Clinton was also quiet on matters pertaining to religious liberty. While she paid lip service to the idea whenever Trump made comments about barring Muslims from coming into the country, she never addressed the religious liberty issues facing many evangelicals. This was especially the case with marriage. Granted, evangelicals should not have expected Clinton to defend traditional marriage or promise to help overturn *Obergefell v. Hodges*, but she did not seem willing to support something akin to what law professor and author John Inazu has described as "confident pluralism."[39] The question of how to make room for people with religiously motivated beliefs that run contrary to the ruling in *Obergefell* is still being worked out, and the question is not an easy one to parse. But when Hillary claimed that her candidacy was a candidacy for "all Americans," it seemed like an attempt to reach her base, not to reach across the aisle. Conservative evangelicals were not buying it.

In the choice between the strongman who paid lip service to protecting their values and their age-old enemy in the culture wars, many evangelicals insisted they had no choice but to stick to the playbook. After one of my recent lectures on Trump and his evangelical supporters, a woman approached me at the lectern and identified herself as an evangelical who voted for Donald Trump. "I am part of the 81 percent," she said, "but what choice did I have?" With pundits and polls predicting a narrow win for Clinton right up until Election Day, it seemed that every vote that was not cast for Donald Trump would be a vote for Hillary Clinton and what seemed like a juggernaut—in the White House and the Supreme Court—that would steamroll their long-cherished values. While many of Trump's evangelical opponents said that they could not tell their children or grandchildren that they voted for such a moral monster, other evangelicals were saying exactly the same thing about voting for Hillary Clinton. On Election Day, long-held fears or threats whose specter had been stoked for decades simply could not be overcome.

CHAPTER 3

A SHORT HISTORY OF EVANGELICAL FEAR

True religion, I believe, begins in doubt and continues in spiritual exploration. Debased religion begins in fear and terminates in certainty.

— Neal Gabler[1]

Despite the biblical passages exhorting followers of Christ to "fear not," it is possible to write an entire history of American evangelicalism as the story of Christians who have failed to overcome fear. Evangelicals have worried about the decline of Christian civilization from the moment they arrived on American shores in the seventeenth century. They have celebrated American values such as "freedom" and "liberty" while simultaneously building exclusive communities that do not tolerate dissent. They have revealed their fear in the ways they have responded to the plight of people who do not share their skin color. White evangelical fear of newcomers—those who might challenge the power and privilege that evangelicals have enjoyed in a nation of Protestants—has been present in every era of American history. In a sin-cursed world, we should expect anxiety-induced emotions to rise in response to social change. But evangelicals have not always managed their fears in a healthy way. Their responses have led to some dark moments in the history of American Christianity and, indeed, the nation.

Fear in the City on a Hill

On January 11, 1989, in his farewell speech before the nation, President Ronald Reagan expounded on his understanding of American identity:

> I've spoken of the shining city all my political life, but I don't know if I ever quite communicated what I saw when I said it. But in my mind it was a tall, proud city built on rocks stronger than oceans, wind-swept, God-blessed, and teeming with people of all kinds living in harmony and peace; a city with free ports that hummed with commerce and creativity. And if there had to be city walls, the walls had doors and the doors were open to anyone with the will and the heart to get here. That's how I saw it, and see it still.

It was a powerful and heartfelt message from a popular American president who had always been supportive of the Christian Right's political agenda. During his presidency he regularly used the phrase "shining city on a hill" as a metaphor for American exceptionalism. The reference came straight from Jesus's words in the Sermon on the Mount: "Ye are the light of the world. A city that is set on a hill cannot be hid. Neither do men light a candle, and put it under a bushel, but on a candle-stick; and it giveth light unto all that are in the house. Let your light so shine before men, that they may see your good works, and glorify your Father which is in heaven" (Matt. 5:14-16).

Reagan and his speechwriters also knew that "city on a hill" (the president added the word "shining" for greater rhetorical effect) was used in another sacred text of American civil religion—John Winthrop's 1630 lay discourse "A Model of Christian Charity." We don't know whether Winthrop ever actually delivered this speech, but he probably *wrote* it aboard the *Arbella* as he traveled westward across the Atlantic with persecuted English Puritans seeking new opportunities in North America. When the ship landed in the port of Salem on June 12, 1630, Winthrop officially became governor of the Massachusetts Bay Colony. It is doubtful that Reagan knew very much about John Winthrop or the Puritans, but many of his followers on the Christian Right wanted to reclaim the spiritual principles that Winthrop prayed would become the bedrock of his new "city." The idea of the United States as a shining beacon of power, light, and freedom seemed to best explain its divine mission to make the world safe for democracy and its obsession with ending totalitarian regimes abroad. John Winthrop's colony was, of course, hardly an example of "harmony and peace." The doors of the new "city" were seldom "open to anyone." And very little about everyday life in Massachusetts Bay looked like the United States in the 1980s. But it didn't matter: this is how Reagan saw it, and his evangelical followers on the Christian Right saw it the same way.

In his masterful treatment of the use of "City on a Hill" in the history of American rhetoric, historian Richard Gamble reminds us that Winthrop used the phrase to explain the belief that Massachusetts Bay, as a new Israel, enjoyed a special relationship with God. Rather than triumphantly announcing that the colony would be a beacon of light to the rest of the world—a shining model for others to follow—Winthrop's discourse was more a proclamation that the stakes couldn't possibly be higher for the new colony. If the colonists did not lead lives of Christian service to God and their fellow believers, or if they failed to make every effort to build the body of Christ through the winning of new converts, the Lord would be displeased. But if they did meet God's requirements in these areas, he would bless them and their society. Ancient Israel had failed to live up to God's standards; it was now time for the Puritans of Massachusetts Bay to try to do better. And the stakes were not only divine in nature; Winthrop let them know that the world was watching their North American experiment. If they botched it, they would be a laughingstock. This covenant relationship with a sovereign and all-powerful God gave the Puritans a "heavy weight of responsibility."[2]

Winthrop did not hesitate to use the fear of God to motivate his charges to fulfill their covenantal responsibilities. The Puritans, of course, knew the problems with such a claim. They knew that "the church was transcendent and universal, drawn from every nation and language, and not provincial." Yet, contrary to traditional Calvinist theology, Winthrop made it clear in "A Model of Christian Charity" that when the Puritans landed in Massachusetts, God's "chosen people and Promised Land became earthly." The result, according to Gamble, was a "civil religion at odds with a Christian understanding of the church."[3]

On the surface, Winthrop's efforts to put the fear of God into the settlers of Massachusetts was very close to what the Bible teaches about fear. In the preceding chapter we saw that the only appropriate kind of fear for Christians is the fear of a holy and righteous God, who will one day judge his creation. The Puritans understood this kind of fear better than most. But when such appeals to the fear of God were used to sustain a rightly ordered society, they inevitably led the Puritans down some destructive paths, especially destructive for those who claimed the name of Christ and their adherence to New Testament faith.

The Bible was indispensable to the maintenance of Winthrop's vision. The Puritans of Massachusetts Bay were people who had the freedom to read the Bible for themselves; yet they were required by their society to interpret it in the correct way. The Puritans used the word "orthodoxy" to describe the proper interpretation of Scripture and the theology that emanated from it. Massachusetts Bay would be a godly commonwealth where Puritan orthodoxy informed the legal code and where the line between church and state was very thin. The defense of orthodoxy was directly linked to the keeping of the covenant and, consequently, the survival of the city on a hill.

Yet this special covenant with God was not easy to keep for Calvinists, with their robust view of human depravity. In fact, the spiritual decline of the colony probably began before the *Arbella* arrived on New England's shores.[4] If we listen to today's conservative evangelical politicians and pseudohistorians, Massachusetts Bay was a place where the seeds of a great Christian nation were planted and grown: it was a community in which religious liberty was born and American exceptionalism was nourished. But actually the story of Massachusetts Bay is the story of a group of devoted Puritans desperate to preserve a Christian civilization that would never be able to measure up to their own standards of success, or to the definition of what it meant to be Christian. It is the story of a group of Bible-believers who lived in fear of what a wrathful God might to do them if they failed to keep their society pure. They were thus remarkably willing to believe that their society was in a constant state of decline. This was arguably the first American evangelical fear.

The demands of the covenant made the Puritans anxious about every moral failure—personal and collective—that they were able to diagnose. Puritan magistrates and clergy spent most of the seventeenth century complaining about profane activities that triggered God's displeasure. The list of social sins was long: it included disorderly speech, crime, idleness, contempt for authority, intemperance, gambling, and adultery.[5] Educated ministers worried that orthodoxy did not always trickle down to the people who sat in their pews. Historians have shown that those living in that colony, even church members who claimed to have had a conversion experience, practiced a mixture of Christianity, magic, and other folk practices.[6]

Members of Massachusetts society who posed serious threats to orthodoxy were removed from the colony. Some were even executed. Anne Hutchinson, for example, accused clergymen of teaching salvation by works (a "covenant of works") and claimed to receive direct revelation from God. The fact that she taught theology to men in a way that was "not fitting" for her sex did not help her case in this patriarchal society. Hutchinson's courageous efforts to follow her conscience on religious matters resulted in her banishment from the colony. Members of the radical sect called the Society of Friends (Quakers), with their aggressive proselytizing and their claim that God spoke to them directly, posed an even graver threat to the social order of the city on a hill. Between 1659 and 1661, four Quakers—the so-called "Boston martyrs"—

were executed for their religious beliefs. Unlike other British colonial experiments in North America, such as Rhode Island, Pennsylvania, and New Jersey, the Puritans of Massachusetts Bay allowed their fear of religious diversity and their dogged defense of one specific reading of the Bible to lead them, ironically, toward intolerance.

Puritan fears were also on display in their relationship with the Native Americans who lived in the Massachusetts Bay Colony. Conflict with Indians on the frontier was common in seventeenth-century New England. Some ministers believed that Indians represented the most concrete example of Satan's efforts to destroy the city on a hill. According to this line of thinking, the century's two major Indian wars—the Pequot War in 1637 and King Philip's War in 1676—were punishments from God for the Puritans' failure to uphold their end of the covenant. Frontier missionaries, such as John Eliot and Daniel Gookin, established communities of "praying Indians," but their efforts drew little attention from the powerful clergy who presided over the colony's most influential churches. In fact, the evangelization of Indians often exacerbated already existing Puritan fears about Native Americans. When missionaries tried to convince their fellow Puritans to accept Indian converts as part of the religious and social life of the Bay Colony, or to trust them as political and military allies, their efforts did not get very far. The integration of Christian Indians into Massachusetts society was not an option that many Puritans were willing to entertain. As Puritans became more acquainted with Indian converts in their midst, the racial differences between the groups intensified in spite of the fact that both European and Native Puritans shared an orthodox belief and saw the necessity of godly living.[7]

By the end of the seventeenth century, Winthrop's city on a

hill seemed to be under threat. Massachusetts' participation in the ever-expanding British transatlantic marketplace brought materialism and economic acquisitiveness to the colony. It also brought "strangers," who had no stake in the religious ideas at the heart of this colonial experiment. These strangers preferred the rough culture of the port towns and their taverns over the spiritual life offered to them in the meetinghouse. They seemed to be motivated less by a commitment to the common good (as the Puritans understood it) and more by the individualism and greed associated with commercialism. The number of religious conversions in the colony had declined to such an extent that the magistrates and clergy needed to come up with new ways of defining church membership that did not require members to testify to a born-again experience. As Massachusetts opened up to the rest of the English-speaking world, talk of a covenant relationship between the colony and God became more confined to Sunday morning services. In 1684, the English government revoked the charter of the Massachusetts Bay Colony, effectively ending its legal power to shape its own destiny as a godly commonwealth.

Puritan fears about the moral and spiritual decline of their society reached a zenith in 1692. In that year 160 men and women in the colony were accused of witchcraft. Nineteen people were executed by public hanging, and one was pressed to death. The Puritan belief in Satan, demons, and witches only partly explains what happened in Salem and the surrounding towns. New England had seen its share of witch trials over the decades, but the region had not experienced such a scare in more than thirty years. This fact has prompted historians to ask questions about the timing of the witchcraft accusations and why they spread so quickly. Historians of both colonial America and early modern Europe have argued convincingly that witch trials were means by which religious and political leaders dealt with men and women who posed a threat to traditional Christian societies. Many of the Massachusetts residents who were accused by their neighbors of witchcraft—and the clergy and prominent lay leaders who supported those accusations—believed that the outbreak of malfeasance was a clear sign that Satan was trying to deal a deathblow to their godly commonwealth. During the trials, Salem minister Samuel Parris preached from Revelation 17:14, reminding his congregation that "the Devil and his instruments will be warring against Christ and his followers." He continued: "There are but two parties in the world . . . the Lamb and his followers, and the dragon and his followers. . . . Everyone is on one side or another." This would not be the last time we would witness this kind of dualistic thinking or sense of theological certainty. In fact, as we shall see, it would become a hallmark of evangelical thinking.[8]

The Salem witch trials were a disaster for Massachusetts Bay. Despite warnings from some of the colony's most prominent ministers, the magistrates used spectral evidence (dreams or visions of witches visiting people in the night and causing or threatening harm) to convict the accused witches and sentence them to death. The speed with which the witchcraft allegations spread throughout northeast New England is evidence of how Christians allowed fear, based on sketchy evidence, to consume them.

After the hysteria came to an end, many of the participants in the witch trials looked back with embarrassment. Some asked for forgiveness or made public testimonies of repentance. In 1695, Thomas Maule, a member of the Society of Friends in Salem, wrote a tract denouncing his Puritan neighbors for their un-Christian behavior during the witchcraft frenzy. In *Truth Held Forth and Maintained*, Maule declares: "For it were best that one hundred witches should live, than that one person be put to death for a Witch, which is not a witch."[9] Maule's words were a stinging and prophetic critique of the Salem witch trials; they also landed him in jail for twelve months.

The Catholic Menace

There were few Catholics in early New England, but that did not prevent the Puritans from fearing them and what they could do to the eternal souls of their loved ones. As descendants of the Protestant Reformation, Puritans were convinced by their reading of the Bible that Catholicism was a false religion. New England clergy equated "popery" with the "great whore of Babylon" who was prophesied in the book of Revelation. The Puritans believed that Protestantism, when compared to Roman Catholicism, was a religion of liberty; Protestants could read the Bible for themselves in the vernacular language; they were free from the "superstitions" of the Catholic mass; and they were not restricted in their worship by the sacramental and liturgical trappings that held ordinary Catholics in a state of spiritual tyranny. Finally, Protestants believed that salvation came through faith alone and not by good works. They were sure that Catholics would spend eternity in hell.

Throughout the colonial era, thousands of Catholics— both European and converted Native Americans—lived to the north of the British colonies in the settlement of New France. Puritans knew that the Jesuit clergy of these Catholic settlements regularly outdid them in their attempts to convert the

Indians. The eighteenth-century wars between the British colonists and the French for control of North American territory were, in the minds of New Englanders, nothing short of religious wars. They lived under constant threat of raids on Puritan villages that were carried out by Indians allied with the French. An entire genre of literature known as "captivity narratives," written by men and women who had been seized by Indians during these attacks, described Jesuit attempts to convert Puritan captives to Catholicism. In 1704, during Queen Anne's War, Mohawk Indians raided the frontier Massachusetts town of Deerfield. They murdered fifty inhabitants of the village and kidnapped over one hundred more. One of the Puritans taken was Eunice Williams, the daughter of Rev. John Williams, the town's Puritan minister. Perhaps the most revealing part of the Williams family story, as told by historian John Demos, is that Rev. Williams, while certainly concerned about his daughter's physical safety, was more fearful about the eternal state of her soul after he learned that she had converted to Catholicism.[10]

By the mid-eighteenth century, anti-Catholicism was rampant up and down the Eastern Seaboard. Small communities of Catholics worshiped freely in most of the colonies, and some of them would make significant contributions to public affairs. But everyone understood that it was Protestantism, not Catholicism, that represented the future of British provincial life. The Protestant culture of British America intensified during the evangelical revivals that swept through the colonies in the 1740s. To many Protestants, the revivals were an outpouring of the Holy Spirit; that, in turn, was a sign of divine favor toward the British Empire and clear evidence that God was on the side of Protestantism. The spiritual power of these revivals, which historians have described collectively as the First Great Awakening, served as a bulwark against the influence of Catholicism.[11]

The final eighteenth-century war for the North American empire—the French and Indian War—brought anti-Catholic sentiment in the colonies to a fever pitch. Samuel Davies, a leader of the evangelical movement in Virginia and at that time the president of the College of New Jersey at Princeton, claimed during the war: "I would rather fly to the utmost end of the earth, than submit to French tyranny and Popish superstition." During the same year, Esther Edwards Burr, the daughter of revivalist Jonathan Edwards and the mother of future vice president Aaron Burr, wrote to her friend Sally Prince in Boston: "You can't conceive my dear what a tender Mother undergoes for her children at such a day as this, to think of bring[ing] up Children to be *dashed against the stones by our barbarous enemies*—or which is worse, to be inslaved by them, and obliged to turn *Papist*." Following the British victory at Fort Louisburg in 1758, evangelical clergyman Thomas Prince was delighted that "a great support of Antichristian Power is taken away, and the visible Kingdom of God enlarged."

During the French and Indian War, anti-Catholicism in the colonies took on a decidedly political flavor. Catholicism not only became synonymous with the political tyranny of France under the Bourbon kings; it also became associated with savagery, ignorance, and any government effort to threaten religious or political liberty. Having been aroused against the tyranny they saw in the Catholic French, colonists could now easily make the leap to see such tyranny in the British king and Parliament during the American Revolution. Thomas Paine, in his popular tract *Common Sense*, tried to convince ordinary colonists to rebel against the British crown by claiming that "monarchy in every instance is the Popery of government."[12]

The American alliance with France during the Revolution did not bring an end to anti-Catholicism in the newly formed United States, but it did curb it significantly. As we shall see below, American evangelicals became more concerned in these years about the threat that deism and unbelief might have on their burgeoning Christian republic. It was not until after the War of 1812, when large numbers of Irish and German Catholic immigrants began arriving in the United States, that anti-Catholic sentiment returned with force. This later attack on Catholics coincided with another series of evangelical revivals, commonly referred to as the Second Great Awakening. The revivals also led to the initiation of reform movements whose goal was to sanctify the nation. Some of those influenced by the revivals put their faith into action by promoting temperance, opposing slavery, endorsing new rights for women, and establishing benevolent societies and schools to teach evangelical Christianity to children, distribute Bibles, and educate Americans about the importance of the Sabbath. The revivals were a potent mix of spiritual dynamism, moral reform, and newly fueled suspicions of religious outsiders.[13]

One of the leaders of this second great era of revival and reform also happened to be one of the strongest anti-Catholic voices in America. Lyman Beecher, a well-known New England Congregationalist minister, became the first president of Lane Theological Seminary, an evangelical training school for ministers in Cincinnati that was committed to the Protestant reform of society. On a fundraising visit to Boston in 1834, Beecher delivered a speech, entitled "Plea for the West," which began with American exceptionalism. Beecher believed that the United States was a Protestant nation with a special mission from God to spread liberty and democracy around the world. He affirmed Jonathan Edwards's view that the Second

Coming of Jesus Christ would take place in the United States, but this essential moment in evangelical eschatology would only commence in America if "evangelical light" continued to win the cultural battle against the dark forces of "superstition." Beecher thought that the advancement of America as a Protestant republic depended on the education of citizens in "intelligence," "moral principles," and "patriotism." He estimated that there were 1.5 million children in the developing "West" who lacked proper education, thus making them susceptible to "danger" from the "rapid influx of foreign emigrants, unacquainted with our institutions, unaccustomed to self-government, inaccessible to education, and easily accessible to prepossession and inveterate credulity and intrigue, and easily embodied and wielded by sinister design."[14]

Lest anyone who heard or read "Plea for the West" (printed in 1835) did not know that Beecher was referring to Catholics when he talked about immigrants "wielded by sinister design," he spent the rest of his speech explaining Catholicism's threat to the American republic and instilling in his hearers and readers the fear of a potential Catholic takeover of their beloved Protestant nation. Beecher says that Catholics had the right to come to America and worship according to the dictates of their consciences. They should thus be treated warmly, with "words and acts of kindness," lest they grow in their hatred of Protestants. But Beecher is more concerned with the "political claims and character" of the Catholic religion. Catholics thrive, he argues, in a "church and state alliance with the political and ecclesiastical governments of Europe hostile to liberty." He continues:

[I]f Catholics are taught to believe that their church is the only church of Christ, out of whose inclosure none can be saved,—that none may read the Bible but by permission of the priesthood, and no one be permitted to understand it and worship God according to the dictates of conscience, that heresy is a capital offense not to be tolerated, but punished by the civil power with disenfranchisement, death, and confiscation of goods—that the pope and the councils of the church are infallible, and her rights of ecclesiastical jurisdiction universal, and as far as possible and expedient may be of right, and ought to be as a matter of duty enforced by the civil power,—that to the pope belongs the right of interference with the political concerns of the nations, enforced by his authority over the conscience of Catholics. . . . If these things are so, is it invidious and is it superfluous to call the attention of the nation to the bearing of such a denomination upon our civil and religious institutions and equal rights?[15]

There was some truth to Beecher's claims. He provided evidence of bishops in western Ohio and Kentucky who wanted to convert Protestants to Catholicism and "destroy the influence" of their denominations on the frontier. American evangelicals like Beecher were also aware of papal pronouncements condemning American and British Bible societies and forbidding Catholics to read and interpret the King James Bible. The chances that Catholicism would ever overrun the Protestant culture of the United States were slim, but it did not appear that way to Beecher as he watched Catholics populate the West.

Beecher rails against the impending danger of Catholic immigration. He claims that "since the irruption of the northern barbarians the world has never witnessed such a rush of dark-minded population from one country to another, as is now leaving Europe and dashing upon our shores." He describes Irish and German Catholic immigrants to America as a "coming evil" and compares them to the locusts of Egypt that are described in the book of Exodus. "For the causes are mighty and radical which threaten us," Beecher complains, "should we shut our eyes and stop our ears, and cry, Peace, while destruction is coming?" He ends his speech by calling on the United States government to institute a plan of immigration restriction: "Ought there not to be a governmental supervision of the subject of immigration, which shall place before the nation, annually, the number and general character of immigrants . . . ?" When Beecher uses the phrase "general character," he means "Catholic."[16]

Whether they read Beecher or not, evangelical Christians acted upon their fear of Catholic immigrants. During the three decades leading up to the Civil War, anti-Catholicism mobilized evangelicals to get involved in politics, many for the first time in their lives. As historian Richard Carwardine has shown, evangelical anxieties about the excessive use of alcohol, the end of slavery, or the decline of the Christian Sabbath paled in comparison to their "uninhibited anti-Catholicism." Evangelicals who worried about the Catholic menace—both men and women—gravitated toward the Whig Party in the 1830s. Most Whigs were ardent nationalists who worked to build a homogeneous Protestant culture. The Whigs' political opponents, the Democrats, favored individual liberty on moral issues and championed religious diversity. While the Democrats did attract some working-class evangelicals, many middle-class evangelicals refused to support the party of Andrew Jackson, Martin Van Buren, James K. Polk, and Franklin Pierce because it catered to the interests of Irish-Catholic immigrants. Like Beecher, white middle-class evangelicals believed that the nation was engaged in a spiritual battle between the forces of God and the forces of evil. These "dualistic, Manichean patterns of thought," Carwardine writes, provided the "philosophical legitimacy for political restrictions on Catholics and foreigners." It was a nativist impulse, he says, that "hinted at paranoia."[17]

In the 1850s, white evangelical fear of Catholic influence led many evangelicals to find a home in the newly formed American, or "Know-Nothing," Party. The Know-Nothing Party was built on the belief that America was a Protestant nation. Its 1856 platform called for the repeal of naturalization laws, a "war to the hilt on political Romanism," a "hostility to all Papal influence," the "amplest protection of Protestant Interests," the opposition to "foreigners" in the military, more "stringent & effective" immigration laws, the "formation of societies to protect American interests," and "death to all foreign influences."[18] The Know-Nothings drew their greatest strength from nativist white evangelicals, especially Methodists, Presbyterians, Baptists, and Congregationalists. One contemporary report claimed that two-thirds of Methodist clergy in Indiana supported the Know-Nothing platform. A popular Methodist journal, the *Southern Christian Advocate*, described the emergence of the Know-Nothings as a "strange and wonderful" development, while other evangelicals attributed the party's success to divine providence. Evangelical clergy who aligned with this xenophobic party often turned their backs on the long-standing belief that ministers should not engage in partisan politics. They joined the Know-Nothings in the hope that their anti-Catholicism might allow them to gain influence and power in their communities and states. Not all evangelicals supported the Know-Nothings. Some believed that a political party devoted to anti-Catholicism might strengthen Rome's interest in America. Others argued against Know-Nothing ideology with appeals to the human dignity of immigrants or the belief that the United States was an asylum that welcomed strangers so that they could peacefully assimilate them to American (Protestant) values once they arrived. Still, the Know-Nothings had plenty of evangelical support.[19]

Fearing the Infidel

In the years prior to the Civil War, American evangelicals fought a two-front battle in defense of a Protestant nation. Catholicism was portrayed as a real and imminent threat to the survival of the republic, but so were unbelievers, deists, skeptics, freethinkers, atheists, universalists, and other assorted heretics searching for a place in the religious makeup of the nation.[20] Evangelicals most frightened by the presence of these so-called infidels could be found everywhere, but many of them eventually gravitated toward the Federalists, a party whose members wanted to build a strong central government capable of curbing the passions of ordinary people and defending the Christian roots of a moral republic.[21]

Elias Boudinot, a prominent evangelical Federalist and a former president of the Continental Congress, compared the United States to two of the Asia Minor churches described in the third chapter of the book of Revelation. Like the New England Puritans who came before him, Boudinot was convinced that if Americans remained obedient to God and the Bible, the nation would end up like the Church of Philadelphia, a congregation praised for its faithfulness. But if America did not take seriously the teachings of Christianity, it would end up like the Church of Laodicea, a congregation that had "lost its first love." Because the Laodicean church was neither "hot nor cold," God declared that he would "spew thee out of my mouth." Between 1790 and 1815, Boudinot and his Federalist colleagues, as well as many American evangelicals, feared that they were in danger of moving from the privileged position of the Church of Philadelphia to the condemned status of the Church of Laodicea. They often expressed their anxiety in their staunch criticism of political figures and public intellectuals, including the president of the United States, who offered the American people an understanding of human history driven by secular progress rather than the hope of Jesus Christ's return.[22]

Some evangelical Federalists dabbled in conspiracy theories. In 1798, Jedidiah Morse, the congregational minister in Charlestown, Massachusetts, and a well-known author of geography textbooks, drew national attention by suggesting that a secret organization called the Bavarian Illuminati was at work "to root out and abolish Christianity, and overturn all civil government." He was convinced that this group of atheists and infidels were behind the secular Jacobin movement in France that sought to purge the nation of organized religion. Morse believed that the Illuminati group was pursuing the same clandestine agenda in America and was working closely with the Thomas Jefferson-led Democratic-Republicans, the Federalists' political rivals, to pull it off. Morse learned about the Bavarian Illuminati from books published in Europe describing a network of secret lodges scattered across the continent. In a 1798 fast day sermon, he appealed to the worst fears of those evangelicals who remained concerned with the moral character of the republic. He described the Illuminati's ominous attempts to "abjure Christianity, justify suicide (by declaring death an eternal sleep), advocate sensual pleasures agreeable to the Epicurean philosophy ... decry marriage, and advocate a promiscuous intercourse among the sexes." The presence of the Illuminati in America should cause Christians to "tremble for the safety of our political, as well as our religious ark."²³ In another sermon on the subject, Morse printed a list of secret societies and Illuminati members currently working their sinister schemes in his Christian nation.

Soon Timothy Dwight, the grandson of Jonathan Edwards and the president of Yale College in New Haven, Connecticut, expressed similar fears about the Illuminati and used his pen to sound the alarm. In a Fourth of July discourse entitled *The Duty of Americans, at the Present Crisis*, Dwight quoted from Revelation 16 to caution his listeners and eventual readers about "unclean teachers" who were educating innocent people in "unclean doctrines." Such teachers were spreading throughout the world to "unite mankind against God." As they performed their malicious work, the Bavarian Illuminati took cues from previous opponents of Protestant America—the Jesuits, Voltaire, and the Masons, to name a few. Dwight called Americans back to God. This, he believed, was the only effective way of resisting such subversive threats to social virtue. "Where religion prevails," he wrote, "Illuminatism cannot make disciples, a French directory cannot govern, a nation cannot be made slaves, nor villains, nor atheists, nor beasts." Dwight reminded his readers that if this dangerous society succeeded in its plans, the children of evangelicals would be forced to read the work of deists or become "concubines" of a society that treated "chastity" as a "prejudice," adultery as virtue, and marriage as a "farce." By the turn of the nineteenth century, news of the Illuminati had traveled up and down the Eastern Seaboard and as far as the Caribbean islands. Boudinot and his fellow Federalist statesman John Jay also bought into this conspiracy theory.

Critics of these evangelical Federalists argued that Morse and Dwight, both clergymen, spent too much time dabbling in politics instead of tending to the souls of the Christians under their spiritual care. Others accused these conspiracy theorists of having "overheated imaginations." Eventually, Morse's accusations against Democratic-Republican societies were unable to withstand the weight of evidence. As historian Jonathan Den Hartog has written, evangelical Federalists concerned about the preservation of a Christian nation "overplayed their hand" by propagating the Illuminati scare. In the process, they "called their standing as societal authorities into question, and ultimately weakened their position" as shapers of American culture.[24]

Anxiety over a secular assault on America's Christian political institutions played a predominant role in the presidential election of 1800. John Adams, the incumbent president, was no evangelical, but as a New England Federalist he defended the idea that republics only survive when built upon the moral foundations of Christianity. His opponent was Jefferson, the vice president of the United States and the politician who, in the minds of evangelical Federalists, was most responsible for allowing infidelity to flourish in America. Jefferson had the support of frontier evangelicals—such as the Methodists and Baptists—who shared his commitment to religious liberty. But the Federalists called attention to his heretical beliefs: Jefferson did not believe in the Trinity, the resurrection of Jesus Christ, or the divine inspiration of the Bible. He was not the kind of leader who should be the president of a Christian nation, the Federalists said, and they were prepared to stage an intense political campaign to discredit him before the American people.[25]

The attacks on Jefferson's supposed godlessness were relentless. William Linn, a Federalist minister from New York, opposed Jefferson's candidacy because of the vice president's "disbelief of the Holy Scriptures . . . his rejection of the Christian Religion and open profession of Deism." Linn feared that, under Jefferson's rule, the United States would become a "nation of Atheists." Linn made clear that "no professed deist, be his talents and acquirements what they may, ought to be promoted to this place [the presidency] by the suffrages of a Christian nation." He even argued that the act of "calling a deist to the first office must be construed into no less than rebellion against God." For Linn, the evangelical choice in the election was clear. If the people were to choose "a manifest enemy to the religion of Christ, in a Christian nation," it would be "an awful symptom of the degeneracy" of America.[26] The political fear-mongering that took place during the 1800 presidential election campaign make the televised attack ads of modern campaigns look tame by comparison. The nation's leading Federalist newspaper, the *Gazette of the United States*, framed the election in stark religious terms by urging readers to ask: "Shall I continue in allegiance to GOD—AND A RELIGIOUS PRESIDENT; or impiously declare for JEFFERSON—AND NOT GOD!" Upon hearing that Jefferson was elected, frightened New England evangelicals thought that the new president's henchmen would soon be coming to their towns and homes on a mission to take away their Bibles.[27]

If Jefferson could use the office of the president to weaken the moral foundation of the United States (such a fear now looks comical, considering that the Second Great Awakening was on its way), as many Federalists believed, Thomas Paine would assist the chief executive in his efforts. In the evangelical mind, Paine had dramatically turned from his status as hero of the American Revolution to one of the new nation's greatest threats. His call for independence in *Common Sense* (1776) had given way to the "infidelity" of *The Age of Reason* (1794), Paine's scathing attack on Christianity. In 1801, Boudinot, fearful that heretics and unbelievers were influencing the faith of America's youth, published a book-length critique of *The Age of Reason* entitled *The Age of Revelation, or the Age of Reason Shewn to Be an Age of Infidelity*. The fact that Boudinot's work appeared shortly after Jefferson's election was no coincidence. The future founder of the American Bible Society was "mortified" when he learned that young people and "unlearned citizens" were reading *The Age of Reason* and giving serious attention to Paine's arguments. Lyman Beecher claimed that rural boys read Paine during their breaks from farm work. Frontier observers noticed that travelers passing through their towns were carrying copies of *The Age of Reason*. Indeed, the book went through twenty-one editions between 1794 and 1800. Boudinot viewed Paine and his writings as an infection slowly eating away at the Protestant culture of the nation. If this metaphor was not convincing enough, he also described *The Age of Reason* as a "flood of infidelity that was deluging our land." Paine's ideas distressed even the most casual American evangelicals.[28]

Racial Fears in the Evangelical South

While the American South was not always the most devout section of the young nation, by the time of the Civil War, 70 to 80 percent of men and women living in the South were evangelical Christians.[29] Most of the population believed that a born-again experience was a prerequisite for eternal salvation; that the Bible was the inspired word of God and the authoritative guide for faith and practice; and that God required Christians to share the good news of Jesus Christ's death, burial, and resurrection with unbelievers. For most of the nineteenth century, Southern evangelicals also had a lot to fear. They worried about whether the nation could survive, to quote Abraham Lincoln, "half slave and half free." Southern soldiers came face to face with the terrors of war, while their loved ones on the home front prayed that they would come home alive. Noncombatants were afraid that the Union army would bring destruction, violence, and bloodshed to their communities. These fears, of course, were not unique to the South; Northerners worried about the same things during the Civil War era. But because of the way the system of labor had developed in the South over the course of the previous two hundred years, its white people faced an additional set of anxieties. These fears centered on the protection of their way of life, a culture and economy built on racial difference and the institution of black slavery.

The Union success in the Civil War was a victory for Northern progress. In the years following the American Revolution, the industrial North developed very differently from the way the agrarian South did. Northerners defended a vision for the nation that was defined by individualism, free labor, market capitalism, manufacturing, and democracy. In this sense, they took pride in thinking that they had evolved beyond the South's backward, traditional, communal, agricultural, and hierarchical society that was sustained by slavery. The South rejected much of this Northern progressive agenda. Democracy, Southerners believed, undermined the conservative social order that God had ordained, and individualism was behind the abolitionist attacks on slavery. Those attacks were the product of ethical thinking detached from a literal reading of the Bible. Abolitionists embraced Enlightenment views of morality that celebrated personal moral preference and the leadings of the human conscience over the clear commands of Scripture. Moreover, the North's move toward manufacturing, Southerners claimed, brought about the exploitation of free labor, the degradation of honest work, and the destruction of the traditional nuclear family.[30]

It was not just Northern progressivism that scared Southern evangelicals. Southerners were caught up in a slave system that kept many of them in a constant state of fear for their lives and the lives of their families. Slave rebellions against white masters were relatively scarce in the antebellum South, but when insurrections did take place, they brought paranoia and panic. Slave revolts—and the potential of slave revolts—filled the collective consciousness of Southerners. When these rebellions or attempted rebellions broke out, as they did in 1800 (Gabriel Prosser), 1822 (Denmark Vesey), 1831 (Nat Turner), and 1859 (John Brown), frightened slaveholders in every instance recalled the horrors of the late-eighteenth-century slave revolt on the French Caribbean island of Saint-Domingue (Haiti). Could such a revolt—celebrated by anti-slavery forces in the Atlantic world for its organization and political success—happen in their own backyard?[31]

Nat Turner's rebellion, which resulted in sixty white deaths in Southampton County, Virginia, was the antebellum South's equivalent to September 11, 2001. The insurrection spread horror throughout the region and had a profound effect on Southern politics and religion. In the wake of the rebellion, Southerners began to fight harder for the expansion of slavery to the west in the belief that its spread to more open country might reduce the proximity of slaves to one another and thus make insurrections more difficult. White churches responded to Turner's rebellion with missionary efforts in the hope that the chances of passion-filled revolts might be reduced if slaves could be monitored more closely by white clergy and lay church leaders.[32] The white evangelical response to Turner's rebellion was strengthened by the rise of abolitionism in the North. Eight months before the Southampton insurrection, Boston's William Lloyd Garrison published his first issue of *The Liberator*, an abolitionist newspaper that called for the immediate emancipation of slaves. Garrison and other abolitionists were successful in using the United States postal system to flood the South with antislavery literature and stoke slaveholders' fears of further rebellions.[33]

The anxieties stemming from slave insurrections led Southern ministers to develop a biblical and theological defense of slavery.[34] These ministers argued that anyone who read the Bible in a literal, word-for-word fashion (as God intended it to be read) would conclude that God had ordained this system of labor. Commonsense interpretations of Bible passages that referred to slavery were often difficult to refute. Old Testament patriarchs such as Abraham owned slaves. Slavery was a legal institution in the New Testament world, and the apostle Paul urged the Roman Christians to obey government laws. In the book of Philemon, Paul required the runaway slave Onesimus to return to his owner. Writing in the immediate wake of the Nat Turner rebellion, Thomas Dew, a professor of political science at the College of William and Mary, used the Bible to defend the view that all societies had a fixed and natural social structure. Citing 1 Corinthians 7:20–21, Dew reasoned that Africans should remain slaves because God had created them to fulfill such a role in society. Slaves had been given a divine "calling" and, in Paul's words, "each one should remain in the condition in which he was called." One South Carolina Presbyterian went so far as to say, "If the Scriptures do not justify slavery . . . I know not what they do justify."[35]

As several careful students of the Southern defense of slavery have shown, though evangelicals turned to the Bible to defend the institution, they often departed from Scripture when making arguments in support of slavery based on race. One could make a strong argument that slavery was condoned by the biblical authors, but it was more difficult to use the Bible to defend white supremacy. Historian Mark Noll has written that "the argument over the Bible and slavery . . . took place in a society where convictions about racial difference . . . affected biblical interpretation at every level." One of Noll's students, Luke Harlow, was more explicit about the role of those convictions: "When applied to a commonsense reading of Holy Scripture, the Bible affirmed what southern white Christians already wanted to believe it said about American race-based slavery."[36]

Evangelicals thought that the South's social order, and its identity as a Christian culture worthy of God's blessing, was grounded in a proper reading of the Bible. In other words, the people of the South—and eventually the Confederate States of America—believed that they were living in a Christian society precisely *because* they upheld the institution of slavery. The abolitionist argument against slavery was not only heretical because it violated the explicit teaching of Scripture; it also threatened the Christian character of the United States. Robert L. Dabney, a Virginia Presbyterian clergyman and one of the strongest defenders of slavery and white supremacy in the South, contended that the notion that slaves—or any Africans, for that matter—had "rights" and thus deserved freedom was a modern idea introduced in the eighteenth century by the progressive thinkers of the Enlightenment, not by the expositors of God-inspired Scripture. Some evangelicals proposed that the unorthodox views of the abolitionists were causing ordinary Southerners to question their belief in an inspired Bible.[37] James Henley Thornwell, another powerful theological voice in support of slavery, understood the Civil War as a clash between atheist abolitionists and virtuous slaveholders: "The parties in this conflict are not merely abolitionists and slaveholders—they are atheists, socialists, communists, red republicans, Jacobins on the one side, and friends of order and regulated freedom on the other." One of Thornwell's students, New Orleans Presbyterian minister Benjamin Palmer, said that the South had been called "to conserve and to perpetuate the institution of slavery as now existing." It was a duty to "ourselves, to our slaves, to the world, and to almighty God."[38]

In their belief that black slaves were inferior to the white inhabitants of the South, evangelicals in the region reflected a common nineteenth-century understanding of race. But the combination of slave rebellions and abolitionist agitation brought this commitment to racial difference even closer to the center of public discourse. Southern evangelicals lived in constant fear of a race war. Because Africans were slaves to their passions, it was thought, they had a natural inclination to steal, lie, and rape. One South Carolina widow claimed to lie in bed each night fearing that at any moment one of her slaves would break into her house and hack her to death with an axe. Historian Charles Dew has made a compelling case that it was white supremacy and the fear of racial mixing that caused the South to secede from the Union. "Our fathers," the Georgia Committee on Secession proclaimed, "made this a government for the white man, rejecting the negro, as an ignorant, inferior, barbarian race." When Confederate leaders floated a proposal to free and arm slaves so that they could fight in the Civil War, opponents of the plan argued that the slaves would run away, join the Union army, and wage war against their owners.[39]

Southern evangelicals also feared the mixing of the races (even though the races were mixed mainly because of the long history of masters raping slaves). Slaveholders believed that their defense of a Christian civilization was directly connected to the purity of the white race. One Presbyterian minister in Kentucky claimed that "no Christian American" would allow the "God-defying depravity of intermarriage between the white and the negro races." South Carolina governor George McDuffie said in 1835 that abolitionists were on a "fiend-like errand of mingling the blood of the master and the slave." In the process, McDuffie argued, they were contributing to the "end of the white republic established in 1776."[40]

Long-standing racial fears did not fade away with the Union victory in the Civil War. Reconstruction amendments that ended slavery (Thirteenth) and provided freedmen with citizenship rights (Fourteenth) and voting rights (Fifteenth) only reinforced Southern racism. A classic example of this was Robert Dabney's opposition to the ordination of freedmen in the Southern Presbyterian Church. During an 1867 debate over this issue, Dabney said that the ordination of African American ministers in the white Presbyterian church would "threaten the very existence of civil society." It was God, Dabney argued, who created racial difference and, as a result, "it was plainly impossible for a black man to teach and rule white Christians to edification." He predicted an ecclesiastical version of "white flight" by suggesting that black ordination would "bring a mischievous element in our church, at the expense of driving a multitude of valuable members and ministers out." Dabney would not sit by and watch his denomination permit "amalgamation" to "mix the race of Washington and Lee, and Jackson, with this base herd which they brought from the pens of Africa."[41]

Throughout the late 1860s and early 1870s, Southerners did everything in their power to win back their region from Radical Republicans who were intent on using the federal government to bring racial equality to the South. They responded with a wave of racial violence directed against black men and women. While white evangelicals may not have universally participated in this white terror, at the very least they did nothing to stop the violence wreaked by the Ku Klux Klan and White Leagues.[42] Fueled by white racism and the Democratic Party, Southerners who exercised violence used the term "redemption" to designate their efforts. Redemption, of course, is a theological word: in the Christian tradition it is used to describe the plan of a gracious God to save humankind from sin through the death of Jesus Christ. In the context of Reconstruction, author Nicholas Lemann reminds us, the word implied a "divine sanction for the retaking of the authority the whites had lost in the Civil War, and a heavenly quality to the reestablishment of white supremacy."[43]

Fundamentalist Fears

Nearly all the anxieties evangelicals faced in the seventeenth, eighteenth, and nineteenth centuries carried over into the fundamentalist movement of the twentieth century. Sadly, the reaction to such fears also remained consistent. In the years between 1860 and 1920, the United States went through some profound changes. The Civil War triumph of Northern capitalism made American industrial power the envy of the world. Major port cities doubled in size, and urbanization extended out to the small railroad villages in the Midwest. Agricultural life did not disappear, but trains shrunk the distance between rural communities and manufacturing centers. The population of the United States tripled in these years, thanks largely to the arrival of more than 28 million immigrants—mostly Catholics and Jews from southern and eastern Europe.[44]

The rise of urbanization, immigration, and industrialization in the decades after the Civil War also came with intellectual changes that posed a direct threat to traditional evangelical beliefs. During the late nineteenth century, the divine inspiration of the Bible, the literal interpretation of the creation story as told in the book of Genesis, and other core Christian doctrines, such as the virgin birth of Jesus and the necessity of a conversion experience, came under attack. German higher criticism—the belief that the Bible was not God-inspired and should be read and interpreted much like any other piece of literature—became ubiquitous in the same American colleges, seminaries, and universities that had once stood as bastions of Christian orthodoxy. Many liberal Protestants were willing to conform their theological convictions to modern culture. These so-called "modernists" rejected the historic doctrine of original sin, celebrated the inherent goodness of human beings, embraced higher criticism, believed that the essence of Christianity was found in service to others rather than in a born-again experience, and understood God "as creator" through the science of Darwinian evolution.

Modernism was one Protestant response to changing times; fundamentalism was another one. By the turn of the twentieth century, conservative evangelicals concerned about these post–Civil War developments had hardened into a full-blown movement ready, to quote one of its leaders, "to do battle royal for the Fundamentals [of the Christian faith]." In the historic Protestant denominations, fundamentalist fear concerning the erosion of Christian orthodoxy resulted in anger and a militant opposition to modernism. Anyone who attended a Billy Sunday crusade could hear the former major-league baseball player defend the historic evangelical commitment to the new birth in one breath and eviscerate the "whiskey gang" and other sources of social immorality with his next breath. William Jennings Bryan, the three-time Democratic Party presidential nominee and the most famous fundamentalist in America, crusaded against the teaching of evolution in the schools. In the end, it was all for naught. The fundamentalists lost control of their denominations and surrendered whatever was left of their nineteenth-century cultural authority and power. Historian William McLoughlin was not too far off the mark when he said that, "by 1915, the modernists were assuming control of the denominations and the seminaries while the fundamentalists rallied vainly around the revivalism of Billy Sunday."[45]

Like evangelicals in other eras, early twentieth-century fundamentalists claimed to have a divine mandate to sustain America's Christian identity. Their defense of traditional Christian doctrine was linked to this larger patriotic mission. Both fundamentalists and modernists believed that the United States was a Christian nation, but unlike the modernists, the fundamentalists' understanding of this identity was bound up with correct theology. The fundamentalists were especially concerned with defending the inspiration of the Bible against the threat of higher criticism. In the process they championed a literal, word-for-word, commonsense reading of Scripture, like the approach taken by proslavery evangelicals in the South. Historian George Marsden has written that, when fundamentalists interpreted the Bible, "they were absolutely convinced that all they were doing was taking the hard facts of scripture, carefully arranging and classifying them, and thus discovering the clear patterns which scripture revealed." For fundamentalists, if the inerrancy of the Bible and other doctrines were to be lost, Christian civilization in America would not have a theological leg to stand on. Since the Bible was the source of all morality, attacks on its authenticity would inevitably lead to social chaos and the eventual collapse of the republic.[46]

Much like their nineteenth-century religious ancestors, fundamentalists were stridently anti-Catholic. The fundamentalist criticism of "modernism" went together well with their disparagement of "Romanism": both "isms" posed a danger to Christian civilization. Fundamentalist pastors taught their congregations to stay out of politics and focus on saving souls or fighting liberal Protestants within the denominations; but they always made exceptions to this rule whenever Catholics ran for office. In 1928, fundamentalists campaigned against Democratic presidential nominee Al Smith, a Catholic who was the four-time governor of New York. Texas fundamentalist J. Frank Norris, who once killed a Catholic businessman who entered his office to complain about his anti-Catholic rhetoric, connected Smith's campaign to satanic forces. New York fundamentalist John Roach Stratton traveled through the South in a failed attempt to persuade Southern Democrats to cast their vote for Republican candidate Herbert Hoover. Anti-Catholicism also motivated fundamentalist support for Prohibition. Catholic immigrants consumed wine and other spirits, so it was no surprise that Billy Sunday used his evangelistic crusades to defend Prohibition and spew anti-immigrant rhetoric.[47]

As we have seen, white conservative evangelicals in the South used the Bible to support slavery, white supremacy, violence against African Americans, and Jim Crow laws. In the process, they had much in common with white Northern fundamentalists. In theory, fundamentalists were aware of the moral problems of racism, but they did very little to bring it to an end. While they did occasionally speak out against lynching and other acts of racial violence, they failed to see how their literal views of the Bible contributed to structural racism in American life. White terror groups seemed to understand this better than the fundamentalists did. As historian Matthew Sutton has shown, the Ku Klux Klan regularly sought partnerships with fundamentalists. The Klan's leaders believed Protestant fundamentalist crusades to save Christian America made them a natural ally in the war against African Americans, Catholics, Jews, and immigrants. Some fundamentalist commentaries on race could have been lifted from the collected works of Lewis Dabney or James Henley Thornwell. A. C. Dixon, the fundamentalist pastor of the Hanson Place Baptist Church in Brooklyn, called the Fifteenth Amendment (the amendment that gave African Americans the right to vote) "the blunder of the age" because African Americans were "ignorant" and thus ill-equipped to cast a ballot. Other fundamentalists upheld typical racial stereotypes that portrayed African Americans as rapists, murderers, and threats to white women. In 1923, *Moody Monthly*, the flagship publication of fundamentalism, published articles defending Klan activity. Fundamentalist fears about the decline of Christian America regularly manifested themselves in racism.[48]

In their search for the theological roots of American fundamentalism, scholars have identified a convergence of two relatively new religious developments: the Holiness movement and Dispensationalism. Evangelicals had always been passionate about personal holiness and piety, and they never wavered in their interest in biblical prophecy; but personal sanctification and the "end times" took center stage in late nineteenth-century evangelicalism and early twentieth-century fundamentalism in a way that they had not done in previous generations. The Holiness movement, which found its roots in the spiritual teachings of John Wesley, was championed in the nineteenth century by Wesleyan ministers and writers such as A. B. Simpson, Asa Mahan, Charles Finney, Phoebe Palmer, and the long list of speakers who came to Holiness camp meetings in the United States and England. The movement emphasized personal sanctification, spiritual purity, and the surrender of one's life to the power of the Holy Spirit. Some adherents of the movement believed that it was possible for a Christian to reach a state of sinless perfection. Fundamentalists often described their pursuit of holiness as the "victorious Christian life." Not all fundamentalists agreed with Holiness teaching, but nearly all of them believed that the spiritual purity of individual Christians was just as important as the doctrinal purity of their beliefs.[49]

The fundamentalist view of personal holiness is partly rooted in admonitions like the one in 2 Corinthians 6:17 (KJV): "Wherefore come out from among them, and be ye separate, saith the Lord, and touch not the unclean thing; and I will receive you." The application of this New Testament verse, and others like it, inspired fundamentalists to separate themselves from worldly activities—smoking, drinking, gambling, movie attendance, and dancing, to name a few—that might cause them to sin. These efforts to shield themselves from the world also applied to intellectual life. Secular universities and colleges taught higher criticism and Darwinism. Philosophy professors challenged fundamentalist belief in the existence of God. The American higher education system, once a stronghold of orthodox belief, had become a den of heresy and religious skepticism. In response to fears that younger generations might be corrupted by worldly pleasures and false doctrine, fundamentalists established their own network of schools. Bible colleges and other fundamentalist educational institutions shielded the faithful from secular temptations that had the potential to undermine their faith. Fear led fundamentalists to separate from the world rather than engaging it. The legacy of the Holiness movement for evangelical intellectual life and cultural engagement has resulted in what Mark Noll described in 1994 as the "scandal of the evangelical mind."[50]

The fundamentalist commitment to a commonsense reading of the Bible—especially passages related to biblical prophecy—contributed to the development of dispensational theology. This is not the place to unpack the intricate history of Dispensationalism, a story that had been told very well by scholars of American religion.[51] But a few words of explanation are necessary. At its core, Dispensationalism divided human history into seven periods. These "dispensations" corresponded with what Scripture revealed about God's design for the ages. Dispensationalists believed God had a plan for both Old Testament Israel and the Christian church (established in Acts 2 when the Holy Spirit descended on the followers of Jesus). Though God was not yet done with Israel, his plan favored Christians—those true believers born again through a conversion experience—over Jews. At the end of human history,

God's agenda for these two groups would come together in the glorious return of Jesus Christ to Jerusalem, the place where he would initiate his millennial kingdom. Believers were exhorted to wait with great anticipation for the imminent "rapture" of the church when Christ would meet them in the air and escort them to paradise. The rest of humanity—the unbelievers—would get another chance to repent of their sins and embrace the message of salvation, but they would have to endure a seven-year period of "tribulation," during which the Antichrist would emerge and lead one final attempt to disrupt God's plan. After the tribulation, Jesus Christ would return with the raptured saints, defeat the satanic forces of the Antichrist at the Battle of Armageddon, and usher in the new heaven and the new earth prophesied in the book of Revelation. Dispensationalists were thus constantly on the lookout for the Antichrist, Satan, and the human forces working to support their evil efforts. Fundamentalist ministers literally tried to scare the hell out of their followers with conspiracy theories about Catholics, communists, modernists, and what one cartoon in a fundamentalist magazine described as "isms of all kinds."

Dispensationalism—and the approach to interpreting the prophetic passages of the Bible that undergirded it—led fundamentalists and their heirs to see the world in black and white. History was best explained as a spiritual battle between the forces of God and the forces of evil. While such a worldview finds support in some teachings of the Bible, fundamentalists all too often showed, and continue to show, supreme confidence in their ability to distinguish between the two forces in every area of life, so that they quickly developed neat categories for good and evil. Historian Doug Frank says: "I tend to think that it was just this quality of dispensationalism—its rationalistic neatness and systematic comprehensiveness—that recommended it to the evangelicals who, during the perilous times at the turn of the twentieth century, were casting about for some means to bring history back under control."[52]

Finally, fundamentalism relied heavily on strong, masculine clergymen. William Bell Riley, John Roach Stratton, Mark Matthews, A. C. Dixon, Reuben Torrey, A. T. Pierson, C. I. Scofield, Arno C. Gaebelein, James M. Gray, Bob Jones, J. Frank Norris, and T. T. Shields were household names in the world of American fundamentalism. These ministers wrote books, preached and published sermons, and founded newspapers and magazines to defend the fundamentals of the faith against modernism. They were also some of fundamentalism's greatest fear-mongers. They gained followers, built large congregations, and gained national reputations by calling attention to the work of the devil in their midst, cultivating anxieties among the faithful about the potential movements of the Antichrist, and sounding the alarm of the modernist threat whenever they saw it rearing its ugly head. These preachers built fundamentalist empires and presided over schools and congregations with the iron hand of biblical truth. They calmed fears by modeling a sense of certainty and authority about the movement of God among his people. Evangelical laypersons turned to these ecclesiastical strongmen to protect them from outsiders, whom they saw as intent on destroying their faith and the Christian identity of their nation. They believed that these outsiders were a threat because their fundamentalist ministers told them so.[53]

As the reader can see, this short history of evangelical fear is actually pretty long—going back to the very establishment of European settlement in America. The various fears that combined to drive white evangelical Christians into the arms of Donald Trump have deep roots in American history. Evangelicals' fears that Barack Obama was a Muslim, and that as president he would violate the Second Amendment and take their guns away, echo—and are about as well founded as— early American evangelicals' fears that Thomas Jefferson was going to seize believers' Bibles. The Christian Right's worries in the 1960s and 1970s that they might lose their segregated academies should take us back to the worries of white evangelicals who lived in the antebellum South. Contemporary efforts to declare America a Christian nation should remind us of similar attempts by fundamentalists a century ago. Efforts to portray immigrants—documented and undocumented—as threats to white Christian culture take us back to the days of evangelical support for the Know-Nothing Party and the nativist outbursts of Lyman Beecher.

This is the historical context that white evangelicals in America have inherited. We have been here before. In some sense, we have never left.

CHAPTER 4

THE COURT EVANGELICALS

Let him begin by treating the Patriotism . . . as part of his religion. Then let him, under the influence of partisan spirit, come to regard it as the most important. Then quietly and gradually nurse him on to the state at which the religion becomes merely a part of the "cause," in which Christianity is valued chiefly because of the excellent arguments it can produce. . . . Once [he's] made the world an end, and faith a means, you have almost won your man, and it makes very little difference what kind of worldly end he is pursuing.

— Screwtape to Wormwood,
C. S. Lewis, *The Screwtape Letters*

I n his book *The Origins of Courtliness,* historian Steve Jaeger retells a story told by the eleventh-century church reformer Petrus Damiani.

A cleric of the church of Cologne is fording a river, when suddenly a man appears next to him, takes hold of the reins of his horse, and stops him. It is Saint Severin, once archbishop of Cologne, now a spirit wandering the earth. The cleric, struck dumb by the apparition, recovers sufficiently to ask what so famous a man is doing in this sorry place. "Take my hand," the saint replies, "and you will learn my story by feeling rather than by hearing." They clasp hands and proceed. But the cleric at once notices that the saint's hand is hot. The heat increases and becomes so intense that the flesh begins to melt away. Soon the cleric holds in his hand only bare bones with small pieces of flesh clinging to them. "Why is so terrible an affliction visited on a man so revered by the church?" he asks. The saint replies that only one thing was found punishable in him: that as a cleric at the king's court, he took so keen an interest in the affairs of the state that he neglected chanting the liturgy at the prescribed hours. For this sin he now suffers, and he begs the cleric and his fellows to pray for him so that he can be redeemed and enter heaven.[1]

Damiani's story (as translated by Jaeger) sheds light on a common problem for late medieval clergymen with access to political power. The king's court was a dangerous place, even for the most devout and pious members of the clergy. The courtiers who served in the court had one primary goal: to gain access to and win the favor of the monarch. They could do this through their knowledge of military strategy, their grasp of the liberal arts, or simply by the way they behaved in the king's presence. Such access brought with it privilege and power and an opportunity to influence the king on important matters—if, of course, the king was willing to listen. In his well-known guide to court life, sixteenth-century Italian courtier Baldesar Castiglione described the court as an arena defined by ambition, vanity, and hypocrisy. It was an "inherently immoral" place, a worldly venue "awash with dishonest, greedy, and highly competitive men." One historian has described the courtiers as "opportunistic social ornaments"; another described them as a "chameleons."[2]

If it is not obvious by this point, the skills needed to thrive in the court were different from the virtues needed to lead a healthy Christian life or exercise spiritual leadership in the church. Most courts had their share of clergy, bishops, and other spiritual counselors, but historians agree that the motivations and behavior of these men of the cloth were "hardly distinguishable from the character and obligations of the secular courtiers," men and women whom Damiani described elsewhere as "ruthless, fawning flatterers" in a "theater of intrigue and villainy." A cleric's divine obligation to the church should have softened his devotion to the king, but things rarely turned out that way. Sylvius Piccolomini, the fifteenth-century Renaissance humanist who would eventually become Pope Pius II, was a strong opponent of court clergy. He said that it was very difficult for the Christian courtier to "rein in ambition, suppress avarice, tame envy, strife, wrath, and cut off vice, while standing in the midst of these [very] things. But if any man feels that his God-given talent equips him to conquer them and to stand in fire without being burned, this man I will except from my prohibition on [clerics] serving the court." Pius II doubted that "such a man can exist."[3]

Or consider the words of the thirteenth-century German cleric Hugo Von Trimberg: "Uprightness, decency and truth, humility, modesty and guilelessness, purity, and moderation have been expelled from the court, and in their place exist

lies, deceit, villainy, worthless and knavish character, false-
ness, dissipation, flattery, [and] free-loading . . . and nobody
thinks of God, of salvation and of death."⁴ Indeed, the church
has warned against the pursuit of political power for a long,
long time.

Defending Trump

In the United States we don't have kings, princes, or courts; but
we do have our own version of religious courtiers, and many
of them have what Southern Baptist theologian Richard Land
has gleefully described as "unprecedented access" to the Oval
Office. Disgraced televangelist Jim Bakker, now back with his
own television show after being released from prison, praises
prosperity preacher Paula White because she "can walk into
the White House any time she wants to" and have "full access
to the King."⁵ In the Trump administration, these religious
courtiers are conservative evangelical Christians, well-known
evangelical leaders with very large followings. The roster of
court evangelicals includes Liberty University president Jerry
Falwell Jr., Southern Baptist pastor and Fox News commentator Robert Jeffress, radio host and "family values" advocate
James Dobson, evangelist Franklin Graham, Christian public
relations guru Johnnie Moore (who claims to be a "modern-
day Dietrich Bonhoeffer"), longtime Christian Right political
operative Ralph Reed, culture warrior Paula White, former
presidential candidate Gary Bauer, and megachurch pastor
Mark Burns.

No one is quite sure what kind of role the court evangelicals play in the Trump White House. Some have suggested that
they advise the president on policy issues related to religious

freedom, foreign policy, and judicial appointments. New York City minister A. R. Bernard, who cut ties with Trump in August 2017 after the president refused to condemn the white supremacist rioters in Charlottesville, Virginia, said that evangelicals were not "afforded the proximity to the President" for them to have any real influence. Bernard says that when he signed on to advise the president, he wanted "more than a photo-op." Meetings took place, he said, "but nothing substantive" was discussed.[6] We do know, however, that the court evangelicals like to visit the White House. They flank Trump whenever he signs bills related to issues that matter to them (Robert Jeffress seems to have secured a place at Trump's right hand). They smile for the Oval Office cameras and take selfies that they can share with their social-media followers. On May 3, 2017, the evening before the National Day of Prayer, a group of them had dinner with Trump in the White House. One of the lesser-known court evangelicals, Rev. Greg Lurie, pastor of Harvest Christian Fellowship in Riverside, California, said that he and the rest of the invited guests were "reduced to being like little children" when Trump took them on a tour of the Lincoln bedroom.[7]

Court flattery was on full display when the president gathered his evangelicals to the Oval Office for the signing of a declaration announcing September 3, 2017, as a National Day of Prayer for the people of Texas and Louisiana who were hit by Hurricane Harvey. After signing the bill, Trump asked the court evangelicals to say something. Those in attendance used the opportunity to praise Trump for all he was doing for evangelical causes. Ralph Reed commended him for "acknowledging that God is our source of unity as Americans." Gary Bauer compared Trump to George Washington and thanked him for defending the Judeo-Christian roots of America, alluding to the passage in the Declaration of Independence about rights coming from "our Creator." He then proclaimed America to be a "shining city on a hill." Paula White expressed gratitude for Trump's practice of "calling our nation to God" and for "always" putting "God first." Trump sat at his desk, occasionally nodding in approval, and soaked in the adulation. Jeffress closed the meeting in prayer. He described Trump as a "gift to the country" raised up by God to bring "healing" to a divided America.[8]

Sometimes Trump calls on the court evangelicals to explain to their followers why Trump can be trusted in spite of his moral failings. In a recent convocation at Liberty University, Jerry Falwell Jr. claimed that Trump called him immediately after the infamous Access Hollywood tape was released to the public. The president of the largest Christian university in the world did not go into many details, but he implied that Trump was looking to Falwell for help in smoothing things over with evangelical voters who might be disgusted by these revelations. Falwell Jr. was not only happy to oblige, but he had no qualms about proudly telling the story to thousands of college students gathered in the Liberty auditorium for convocation that day.[9] Falwell also stepped up to the plate for the president after MSNBC "Morning Joe" hosts Joe Scarborough and Mika Brzezinski criticized Trump on the air. When Trump responded with a nasty tweet claiming that during a recent Brzezinski visit to his "Winter White House" in Mar-a-Lago, she was "bleeding badly from a face-lift," Falwell appeared on Fox News and defended the remarks, claiming that "when [Trump] hits them back on Twitter, I actually appreciate that."[10] The court evangelicals even came to Trump's rescue when he drew a moral equivalency between white supremacists in Charlottesville and those who came to the city to try to oppose them. Jeffress went on Fox Business Network and said that Trump "did just fine" in his statement(s) about the event. He then performed a rhetorical move that court evangelicals and other Trump supporters have perfected: he changed the subject and went from defense to offense. Jeffress warned Fox viewers that an "axis of evil" (Democrats, the media, and the "GOP establishment") were plotting to take Trump down. He then reaffirmed America's Judeo-Christian roots without any sense that many of the Judeo-Christian influences that have shaped United States history were intricately bound up with the kind of racism that the nation had witnessed in Charlottesville.[11]

Other court evangelicals may not approve of everything Trump does, but they still believe God has put them in the court for a divine purpose. Richard Land, for example, decided to stay committed to Trump after the president's statements in the wake of Charlottesville because "Jesus did not turn away from those who may have seemed brash with their words or behavior." Land added that "now is not the time to quit or retreat, but just the opposite—to lean in closer."[12] Johnnie Moore also remained with Trump after the Charlottesville comments because "you only make a difference if you have a seat at the table."[13] Perhaps Land and Moore could take a lesson from the evangelical biblical scholar Ben Witherington:

> The sinners and tax collectors were not political officials, so there is no analogy there. Besides, Jesus was not giving the sinners and tax collectors political advice—he was telling them to repent! If that's what evangelical leaders are doing with our President, and telling him when his politics are un-Christian, and explaining to him that racism is an enormous sin and

there is no moral equivalency between the two sides in Charlottesville, then well and good. Otherwise, they are complicit with the sins of our leaders.[14]

Rather than flattering Trump, the court evangelicals should consider the actions of one of King David's court prophets. As recorded in 2 Samuel 12, Nathan took his call from God seriously when he got his "seat at the table." When David committed adultery with Bathsheba and then arranged for her husband, Uriah, to be killed on the battlefield to cover up David's sins, Nathan rebuked his king. He told David the story of a poor man whose beloved "little ewe lamb" was stolen by a self-centered rich man who had plenty of lambs but wanted the poor man's only lamb to serve his guests. When David's anger "was greatly kindled" against the rich man in the story, Nathan said to the king, "You are the man!"

Donald Trump's relationship with some of the court evangelicals can be traced back to a 2011 meeting with evangelical leaders in Trump Tower. Trump was considering a presidential run and wanted to know if he could count on the support of evangelicals, so he asked Paula White to set up the meeting. Trump chose not to seek the presidency in 2012, but he remained connected with many of those evangelical leaders. In September 2015, he again met with evangelical leaders shortly after announcing his candidacy for the GOP nomination. This meeting led to others, all organized by White. During these meetings Trump affirmed his commitment to the issues that evangelicals hold dear: overturning *Roe v. Wade*, defending religious liberty, supporting Israel, and appointing conservative federal judges.[15] Many of those present at those meetings stayed by his side throughout the campaign. Trump rewarded the evangelicals who supported him during the campaign with roles on Inauguration Day. Paula White, Franklin Graham, and prosperity preacher Wayne T. Jackson prayed during the inauguration ceremony. Jeffress preached at a pre-inauguration prayer service at St. John's Episcopal Church in Washington. He used the occasion of his sermon to compare Trump to Nehemiah, the Old Testament leader who helped rebuild the walls of the city of Jerusalem after the people of Judah returned from exile in Persia. Trump was a builder who had been called to the presidency by God in order to build America's decaying infrastructure and construct a wall around the country to keep the nation protected from its enemies.[16]

The New Old Religious Right

The court evangelicals come from three primary streams of American evangelicalism: the Christian Right, the followers of what has come to be known as the "prosperity gospel," and the Independent Network Charismatics (INC). To suggest that there is a "Christian Right" wing of the court evangelical coalition is somewhat misleading, since all the courtiers operate out of the Christian Right playbook (examined at length in chapter 2 above). But Trump's evangelicals have learned from the likes of Jerry Falwell, Pat Robertson, and others that politics is the best way of "reclaiming" the country for Christ. Robert Jeffress, Richard Land, Gary Bauer, and James Dobson have devoted their careers to endorsing political candidates and Supreme Court justices who will restore what they believe to be the Judeo-Christian roots of the country.[17]

Those who make up the Christian Right wing of the court evangelicals defend their support of Donald Trump in a variety of ways. As we have seen, some of them, including Dobson and Falwell Jr., claim that Trump is one of them—an evangelical Christian who has had a born-again experience. Falwell Jr. does not seem particularly concerned about Trump's moral indiscretions; he has even claimed that Trump is the evangelical "dream president."[18] In a speech introducing Trump during a campaign visit to Liberty University, Falwell gushed over the candidate. He praised Trump as a generous man who gave money to those in need. He audaciously invoked Matthew 7:16, the passage in which Jesus tells his disciples that they can recognize a false prophet from a true follower of Christ based on fruits that the true believer will bear. (Trump was a true follower.) Falwell Jr. also informed the Liberty students that in the 1980 presidential election his father, Jerry Falwell Sr., supported Ronald Reagan, a divorced movie star with a pro-choice track record on abortion. The lesson was clear: Christians should simply vote for the candidate who is the best leader. (Of course, as we saw in chapter 2, Falwell Sr. opposed Bill Clinton's presidency because he did not believe Clinton possessed the character necessary to lead the country.) Trump, according to Falwell Jr., was a good businessman and a visionary capitalist. Finally, Falwell Jr. pointed out that Trump, Martin Luther King Jr. (Trump was visiting Liberty University on MLK Day), and Jesus Christ all were persecuted for their "radical" and "politically incorrect" ideas.[19]

Many court evangelicals support Trump because he is "a fighter" who will help them win the culture wars. Very few of them make biblical or theological arguments as to why it is okay for a minister of the gospel to support a man who shows little sign of Christian character. The exception on this front is Robert Jeffress, the pastor of First Baptist Church in Dallas. In May 2016, I debated Jeffress on a National Public Radio program called *Interfaith Voices*. During that debate Jeffress made the following case for why he was morally justified in backing Trump:

> Look, the godly principle here is that governments have one responsibility, and that is Romans 13 [which] says to avenge evil-doers. God gives government the power of the sword, of capital punishment, of executing wrong-doers. He doesn't give you and me those responsibilities or rights individually. So there is a distinction between what the Christian individuals' responsibility is and what government's responsibility is.[20]

Jeffress repeated these ideas several times over the course of the campaign season. In another interview, he described government as a "strongman to protect its citizens against evildoers," adding, "I don't care about that candidate's tone or vocabulary, I want the meanest, toughest son of a you-know-what I can find, and I believe that's biblical." The goal of government, he believes, is to "protect us and leave us alone to practice our faith."[21]

It is worth noting that some very influential Christians through the ages have embraced a view of government close to the Christian libertarianism that Jeffress espouses. For example, Saint Augustine, the fifth-century Christian theologian, argued in *The City of God against the Pagans* (426 CE) that the government is responsible for restraining evil so that Christians can peacefully worship, proclaim the word of God, and participate in the sacraments. Similarly, Martin Luther taught that government, as a secular institution, should be limited to checking sin.[22] And there is a certain consistency in Jeffress's view of government and his support of Trump. His belief that government's sole purpose is to protect its citizens has led him to defend Trump's border wall, oppose the DACA program (the Obama-era initiative that protects illegal immigrants brought to this country as children from being deported to their parents' home country), fight against the taking of innocent life in the womb, argue for the protection of ministers from the IRS through the repeal of the so-called Johnson Amendment, suggest that Muslims should be kept out of the country, prevent homosexual marriages, and claim that Trump has a biblical mandate to kill the leader of North Korea if he poses a threat to United States security. The problem, of course, is that Jeffress defines the evil from which government should protect us according to his own reading of the Bible. In this sense, his view of government departs significantly from the Augustinian/Lutheran view and looks more like the extreme version of Calvinism that informed everyday life in Puritan New England or the medieval Catholic view of government that burned heretics at the stake.

But Jeffress has not always taken this position. As late as 2011, he was hawking a view of government that had less to do with Romans 13, Augustine, or Luther and more to do with the Christian Right playbook. One would have a hard time convincing anyone who has read *Twilight's Last Gleaming: How America's Last Days Can Be Your Best Days* that the Robert Jeffress who wrote that book seven years ago was the same Robert Jeffress who supported Trump in the 2016 GOP primary. For example, early in the book Jeffress chides his conservative evangelical readers for believing that they can "save America" by electing the "right candidates, who in turn will enact the right laws." The minister who invited Fox News host Sean Hannity to speak to his Dallas congregation on a Sunday morning and who appears several times a week as a commentator on that network once told his congregation to "watch cable news less and read their Bibles more to gain God's perspective on the world."[23]

When it comes to voting for political leaders, Jeffress's views have changed a great deal in the past several years. In *Twilight's Last Gleaming*, Jeffress urges his readers to vote for Christian candidates: "If an elected official really believes that he is accountable to God for the decisions he makes," Jeffress writes, "he is less likely to allow external pressure to alter his beliefs." In a very revealing passage, Jeffress says: "Suppose a hostile nation is threatening the security of our country. Would you prefer a president who only looked within himself and to his advisers for guidance? Or would you feel more secure with a president who sought the best counsel of others but also looked to God for direction?" (So much for the "meanest, toughest, son of a you-know-what I can find.") Jeffress also argued that Christians should vote for men of character because a person's "core beliefs serve as a restraint against immorality, corruption, and dereliction of duty." He rejects the "popular" notion that "a politician's personal life has no impact on his public service."

If this is not enough to show how political expediency in the form of Donald Trump has changed Jeffress's theology of government, he spends nearly two pages attacking Martin Luther:

> But what if your choice comes down to voting for a qualified non-Christian or an unqualified Christian? Doesn't competency trump spirituality? Some people quote an alleged comment by Martin Luther: 'I'd rather be ruled by a competent Turk than an incompetent believer.' Such a declaration appears to make

good sense, until you consider some obvious flaws in such an argument.

According to Jeffress, the major "flaw" in Luther's argument is that he believes that a political leader's competence is more important than his character. And speaking of Christian character, he writes that we should not believe a person is an authentic believer because he merely claims (or Paula White claims) to have had a conversion experience. "Beyond a person's words," Jeffress argues, "we must also consider his works."[24]

What is perhaps most disturbing about Jeffress's *Twilight's Last Gleaming* is the way in which his deeply held passion for sharing the gospel of Jesus Christ with others is neutralized by his political agenda. The book begins with a foreword by former Arkansas governor and GOP presidential candidate Mike Huckabee: "If you are looking for a sweet little 'bookette' that is politically correct and safe to read and share with staunch unbelievers so as not to offend them, then put this book down and keep looking." In the first sentence of the first page, Huckabee alienates unbelievers and, in the process, undermines everything Jeffress says in the book about the importance of evangelism. But Jeffress proves in the pages that follow that he does not need Huckabee's help in weakening his gospel witness. Jeffress urges his readers to give up on the culture wars and focus on their "unprecedented chance" in these final days of humankind to "point people to the hope of Jesus Christ." Then he spends the rest of his book teaching his readers how to more effectively *win the culture wars*. At one point in the book Jeffress attributes the steep decline in the number of new converts baptized in the Southern Baptist Church to spiritually weak church members who are afraid to offend anyone with the claims of the gospel. Jeffress may be correct. But the possibility that the decline in baptisms is related to the fact that most Americans now associate the gospel with partisan politics does not appear to have even crossed his mind.[25]

Independent Network Charismatics

The second major stream of court evangelicalism flows from Independent Network Charismatic (INC) Christianity. According to scholars Brad Christerson and Richard Flory, INC is the fastest-growing Christian movement in both the Western world and the global South. INC Christians are outside the network of traditional Pentecostals. While they embrace many of the so-called gifts of the Holy Spirit (tongues-speaking, prophecy, healing, miracles), they do not affiliate with traditional Pentecostal denominations such as the Assemblies of God, the Church of God in Christ, the International Foursquare Gospel Church, or the Church of God (Cleveland, TN). In fact, the INC movement is not a denomination; instead, it is a network of strong spiritual leaders, scattered across the globe, with very large followings. Like the so-called Latter Rain movement that infiltrated traditional Pentecostalism in the 1940s and 1950s, INC leaders believe that a great revival of the Holy Spirit will take place shortly before the Second Coming of Jesus Christ, and God will raise up apostles and prophets to lead this revival. These new spiritual leaders will have authority that comes directly from God, not from denominations or congregations. Some of the more prominent INC prophets, all of whom believe that we are currently living in the midst of this great Holy Spirit revival, include Che Ahn (Harvest International Ministries in Pasadena, CA), Bill Johnson (Bethel

Church in Redding, CA), Chuck Pierce (Glory of Zion Ministries in Corinth, TX), Cindy Jacobs (General International in Red Oak, TX), Mike Bickle (International House of Prayer in Kansas City, MO), Lou Engle (The Call in Colorado Springs, CO), Dutch Sheets (Dutch Sheets Ministries in Dallas, TX), and Lance Wallnau (Lance Learning Group in Dallas, TX).[26]

INC prophets and apostles believe that they have been anointed to serve as God's agents in ushering in his future kingdom, a process that many describe as God "bringing heaven to earth." They are thus deeply attracted to Seven Mountain Dominionism, the belief that Jesus will not return until society comes under the dominion of Jesus Christ. Drawing from Isaiah 2:2 ("Now it shall come to pass in the latter days that the Lord's house shall be established on the top of the mountains"), INC prophets want to reclaim seven cultural "mountains": family, government, arts and entertainment, media, business, education, and religion. The goal is to place God's appointed leaders atop these cultural mountains as a means of setting the stage for the time when God will bring heaven to earth.[27]

In the political sphere, INC prophets promote "kingdom-minded" candidates who will defend Christian values, reclaim the United States as a Christian nation, and ultimately serve as God's instruments for ushering in the kingdom. During the 2016 campaign, several INC leaders endorsed Ted Cruz. In 2012, Cruz's father, Rafael Cruz, a Pentecostal preacher, described his son's election victory in the US Senate race as a direct fulfillment of biblical prophecy. The elder Cruz told a congregation at New Beginnings Church in Bedford, Texas, that God would one day anoint Christian "kings" to preside over an "end-time transfer of wealth" from the wicked to the righteous. After the sermon, Larry Huch, the pastor of New

Beginnings, claimed that Ted Cruz's Senate election was a sign that he was one of those kings. According to his father and Huch, Cruz was anointed by God to help fulfill a major INC prophecy regarding the Christian reclamation of world financial systems. The so-called "end-time transfer of wealth" will relieve Christians of all financial woes, allowing true believers to ascend to positions of political and cultural power.[28]

During the 2016 campaign Mike Bickle, of the International House of Prayer, said that he "didn't have a candidate in mind," but was "praying for [God to place] the right people in the right place."[29] God answered these prayers in the form of Donald Trump. As early as 2007, INC prophet Kim Clement received a word from God: "Trump shall become a trumpet. I will raise up Trump to become a trumpet, and Bill Gates to open up the gate of a financial realm for the church." Early in the 2016 campaign, Lance Wallnau received a similar word: "Donald Trump is a wrecking ball to the spirit of political correctness." When Wallnau's prophecy caught the attention of Trump's evangelical supporters, he was invited to attend a meeting with the candidate and other evangelical leaders in Trump Tower. As Wallnau listened to Trump talk about his desire to give evangelicals a more prominent voice in government, he sensed that God was giving him an "assignment"—a "calling related to this guy." One day, while he was reading his Facebook page, Wallnau saw a meme predicting that Trump would be the "45th president of the United States." God told Wallnau to pick up his Bible and turn to Isaiah 45. On reading the passage, Wallnau realized that, not only would Trump be a "wrecking ball" to political correctness, but he would be elected president of the United States in the spirit of the ancient Persian king Cyrus. In the Old Testament, Cyrus was the secular political leader whom God used to send the exiled kingdom of Judah back to the Promised Land so that they could rebuild the city of Jerusalem and its holy Temple. Wallnau was shocked by this discovery. "God was messing with my head," he told Steven Strang, the editor of *Charisma*, a magazine that covers INC and other Pentecostal and charismatic movements (and claims a circulation of over 275,000). From this point forward, Wallnau would become an outspoken supporter of Donald Trump.[30]

Strang's book on the 2016 campaign, *God and Donald Trump*, provides the best introduction to this wing of court evangelicalism and its apostles who prophesied Trump's election. The book is endorsed by evangelicals on the Christian Right inside and outside the INC movement, including Michelle Bachman, Kenneth Copeland, Robert Jeffress, and Mike Huckabee. In telling the story of the campaign from the INC perspective, Strang claims Trump is a Christian because he opposes abortion, reads the Bible and prays every day, stands up to liberals, defends religious freedom, and believes in the "American Dream." Strang seems to relish the anger displayed by anti-Trumpers in the wake of the election, and his book reads like a Trump victory lap. He accepts Trump's claims of election fraud, attacks Trump's critics for their "divisiveness," labels Trump's opponents "demonic," defends Fox News, and proclaims Trump a "spiritual remedy for America." Cindy Jacobs, the founder of General International and the Reformation Prayer Network, is one of the INC prophets featured in *God and Donald Trump*. In early 2015, Jacobs claimed that God said to her, "I have a trump card in my hand and I'm gonna play it and I'm gonna trump the system." Jacobs did not initially remember the prophecy, but when Trump announced his candidacy, God's words to her became clear. In response, she went to work for Donald Trump. As the general election drew near,

Jacobs led "prayer walks" through seven pivotal swing states. She told Strang that INC leaders around the world—millions of them—were fasting and praying for a Donald Trump victory on November 8, 2016.[31]

The INC prophets and apostles are not as prominent as other court evangelicals, but they have spent time with the president at Trump Tower, the White House, and on the campaign trail. As we have seen, Wallnau was part of Trump's early conversations with evangelical leaders. Jacobs was one of the religious leaders who stood behind Trump on the White House lawn when he announced an executive order on religious liberty on May 4, 2017. Frank Amedia, an INC apostle who claims to have presented Trump with a note at a campaign stop in Youngstown, Ohio, telling the candidate that God had revealed to him that it was a "forgone conclusion" that he would win the GOP nomination, worked as Trump's "liaison for Christian policy." Amedia has led several of these INC leaders in the formation of an organization called POTUS Shield. The clergy associated with this organization gather regularly to pray for Donald Trump to protect him from the Satan-inspired attacks of his political opponents. The POTUS Shield prophets seldom appear at the White House, but they serve as a kind of spiritual support group for God's new Cyrus, who will lead America back to spiritual and economic prosperity and help to set the stage for the dominion of Jesus Christ over all the earth.[32]

The Prosperity Gospel

The third major wing of the court evangelical coalition are the ministers and preachers of the prosperity gospel movement. Historian Kate Bowler has identified four major themes of the prosperity-gospel teaching: faith, wealth, health, and victory. Prosperity preachers teach that faith in God, combined with positive thinking and an optimistic attitude, will ultimately lead to monetary wealth, good health, and victory over the difficult circumstances of life. Bowler writes that prosperity preaching draws on historical Pentecostalism, New Thought (the belief, popular in the nineteenth century, that human beings can heal their bodies through positive thinking), and the "American gospel of pragmatism, individualism, and upward mobility." With the help of television and other forms of media, prosperity preachers such as Kenneth and Gloria Copeland, Oral Roberts, Rex Humbard, Robert Schuller, Jim and Tammy Bakker, Pat Robertson, and Kenneth Hagin gained national attention. The prosperity gospel fell on hard times and lost much of its popularity in the wake of several sexual and financial scandals in the 1980s and 1990s. As the new millennium arrived, however, a host of new preachers took it up and moved into the spotlight. This list of rising stars included Joel Osteen, Benny Hinn, Joyce Meyer, T. D. Jakes, and Creflo Dollar. Perhaps the brightest of them was the court evangelical Paula White.[33]

White's life is a classic rags-to-riches story filled with hardship, struggle, and eventual victory (and wealth) stemming from faith in Christ and positive thinking. She often describes herself as a "messed-up Mississippi girl" whom God saved from an early life of sexual and psychological abuse, poverty, and single motherhood. She is not shy about sharing negative stories from her past because she believes her biography is a testament to how God can help ordinary people live the American dream. As religion scholars Shayne Lee and Phillip Sinitiere note, White preaches a gospel of "redemption and second chances." After a neighbor in her trailer park led her to Christ, Paula married Pentecostal preacher Randy White. The newlyweds scraped together enough resources to start a church in Tampa, Florida, that would eventually become Without Walls International Church. Well before the 2016 presidential election, White was preaching that individuals could make America great again through a combination of faith in God and self-esteem. During one appearance on the Trinity Broadcast Network in 2007, White told her viewers that "anyone who tells you to deny yourself is from Satan."[34]

Lee and Sinitiere call White the "'Oprah' of the evangelical world." In 2001, she began *Paula White Today*, a television show that would soon appear on nine different television networks. Her show and self-help books are filled with helpful advice for overcoming everyday problems. She hawks dietary supplements, teaches her followers how to lose weight (repent and stop eating sugar), and offers beauty tips. According to Lee and Sinitiere, White "reinvented her image with extensive plastic surgery, modish hairstyles, perfectly manicured nails, chic silk suits, fitted dresses, and a leaner size 4 figure." White knows how to market her message and get her followers to send her money. For example, during the 2016 Lenten season, White preached a sermon from John 11:44—the passage in the Fourth Gospel in which Jesus raises Lazarus from the dead. White told her viewers that just as Jesus raised Lazarus, they too could overcome life's difficulties if they would only "sow the seed of faith" in the form of a $1,144 donation to her ministry. White assured her listeners that she does not usually request such specific amounts of money, but this was different. God had specifically instructed her to ask for this $1,144 to correspond with the Scripture passage he told her to preach. Those who donated would receive an anointed "prayer cloth" that would bring "signs and wonders" to their lives. White herself owns a $2.1 million waterfront mansion and a $3.5 million condominium in Trump Tower in New York City.[35]

Over the years several celebrities have become followers of White. When pop icon Michael Jackson was arrested on child molestation charges in 2003, he asked White to come to his ranch and provide him with spiritual counsel. Former New York Mets baseball star Darryl Strawberry sought White's spiritual assistance amid his several stints in prison for drug-related offenses. But White's biggest star-caliber fan is Donald Trump. In 2002, Trump, who had apparently seen White on television, reached out to the popular prosperity preacher and invited her to a meeting at Trump Tower. White and her message must have impressed Trump. Following that meeting they remained friends, and Trump began to take White with him on Atlantic City excursions, where she would conduct Bible studies and prayer meetings with the celebrities who visited his casinos. At some point in their ongoing relationship, White claimed that Trump had a born-again experience. When Religion News Service asked White about Trump's conversion, she said that she was "one hundred percent" sure that he "confesses Jesus Christ as Lord," adding that she "shared the Gospel with Mr. Trump," using the "Romans Road map" (a popular tool used by evangelicals to share their faith with others).[36]

Paula White is not the only court evangelical to come from the ranks of the prosperity preachers. Mark Burns, Darrell Scott, Wayne T. Jackson, and Jentezen Franklin have all made appearances in the White House and have served as surrogates for Trump during and after the campaign. (Burns is perhaps best known for his speech at the 2016 GOP Convention in Cleveland in which he prayed that God would attack the liberal Democrats and protect the GOP against "any attack that comes against us.")

It is not very difficult to find connections between Trump's worldview and the message of the prosperity gospel. Prosperity preachers dress well, have large followings, make effective use of television and the Internet to spread their message, and, as we have seen with Paula White, know how to market themselves. They carry themselves in a professional way and lead their religious organizations with an entrepreneurial spirit. They seem like the kind of people that Trump would not only immediately like, but the kind he would love to have with him in *The Apprentice* boardroom. Furthermore, the core beliefs of the prosperity gospel fit well with Trump's personal creed of success, wealth, and ambition. Much has been made of Trump's experiences in New York's Marble Street Collegiate Church, where, as a child and young adult, he heard uplifting and optimistic sermons from Norman Vincent Peale, the author of *The Power of Positive Thinking*. As Kate Bowler's study makes clear, Peale's blend of Christianity, self-esteem, and popular psychology played an important role in the rise of the prosperity gospel. To put it a different way, it is very unlikely that Donald Trump would be attracted to a form of Christianity that emphasized sin, self-sacrifice, suffering, or anything else that might place demands on his life or prevent him from a pursuit of success as defined by his notion of the American dream. Donald Trump and the prosperity gospel are a perfect match.[37]

The Court Evangelical Agenda

The court evangelicals have decided that what Donald Trump can give them is more valuable than the damage that their Christian witness will suffer because of their association with the president. So what do the court evangelicals want from Donald Trump? It is difficult to find a specific matter of public policy where Donald Trump and the court evangelicals disagree, but much of their support for this president focuses on three things: abortion, religious liberty, and Israel.

Abortion remains at the center of the court evangelicals' political agenda. For many court evangelicals, as we have seen, the 2016 election presented a simple choice: Trump said he would defend the pro-life movement, Hillary Clinton was pro-choice; Trump promised to appoint Supreme Court justices who would challenge—perhaps even overturn—*Roe v. Wade*, and Hillary Clinton would not. When it comes to dealing with the problem of abortion, the court evangelicals have been reading from the same playbook for more than four decades. It teaches them that the best way to bring an end to abortion in America is to elect the right president, who, in turn, will support the right justices. Thus far, things seem to be going well: not only has Trump appointed pro-life justice Neil Gorsuch to the Supreme Court; he has appointed dozens of conservative judges to federal district courts across the country.

Still, it is not exactly clear how this strategy will bring an end to abortion in America. Chief Justice John Roberts, himself a devout Catholic, has called *Roe v. Wade* "settled as the law of the land." And even if *Roe v. Wade* is overturned by the Supreme Court, the issue will be sent back to the states. Abortion is very likely to remain legal in the so-called blue states, including California and New York, and illegal in many of so-called red states, especially in the deep South. State legislatures will need to decide how they will handle the abortion issue in the remaining states, but a significant number of them will probably allow abortion in some form. To put it simply, overturning *Roe v. Wade* will not end abortion in America. It will just make it more difficult for poor women in red states because they will have to travel to a blue state to get an abortion. It may curtail the number of abortions, but it will bring our culture no closer to welcoming the children who *are* born and supporting their mothers.

The taking of a human life in the womb via the practice of abortion is a horrific practice. I believe Christians should be working hard to reduce the number of abortions that take place in the United States—even working to eliminate the practice entirely. But we have been under *Roe v. Wade* for long enough that several generations of Americans now believe that they have a right to an abortion. Such a belief is not going to change anytime soon. Conservative evangelicals and other pro-life advocates spend billions of dollars to get the right candidates elected because they believe that the Supreme Court is the only way to solve the problem of abortion in our society. In 2016, this belief led them straight into the arms of Donald Trump. But what if all the money to support political candidates were to be used in other ways? In a provocative essay directed at evangelicals who voted for Trump because they were pro-life, theologians Stanley Hauerwas and Jonathan Tran offer another approach to this issue that focuses on the witness of church:

> When Christians think that the struggle against abortion can only be pursued through voting for candidates with certain judicial philosophies, then serving at domestic abuse shelters or teaching students at local high schools or sharing wealth with expectant but under-resourced families or speaking of God's grace in terms of "adoption" or politically organizing for improved education or rezoning municipalities

for childcare or creating "Parent's Night Out" programs at local churches or mentoring young mothers
or teaching youth about chastity and dating or mobi-
lizing religious pressure on medical service providers or apprenticing men into fatherhood or thinking
of singleness as a vocation or feasting on something
called "communion" or rendering to God what is God's
or participating with the saints through Marian icons
or baptizing new members or tithing money, will not
count as political.[38]

Religious freedom is another major piece of the court
evangelical agenda. As we saw in chapter 1, things have
changed drastically for conservative evangelicals in the past
decade. By way of several Supreme Court decisions and other
more local developments, the social and cultural views of conservative evangelicals are no longer as culturally ubiquitous
as they once were. They no longer operate from a position in
which their convictions are privileged, which means that they
have been forced to take up the language of religious liberty
(in the way that non-Protestants have done in the United
States for a long time) to keep their views in the public square.

Court evangelicals, for example, believe that a Trump
administration will protect Christian colleges and universities from losing their religious exemptions, exemptions that
allow them to receive federal money despite their religious
opposition to the practice of homosexuality and gay marriage.
One school that would have a lot to lose if these exemptions
were to disappear is Liberty University. Jerry Falwell's school
does not allow faculty members who are gay, and it has taken
strong stances against gay marriage and other related matters
of sexual ethics. In 2015, Jerry Falwell Jr. no doubt had his eye

on the controversy surrounding a bill in the California legislature that would remove Title IX religious exemptions for private liberal arts colleges that are opposed to gay marriage or refuse to hire gay faculty. The sponsors of the bill believed that such rules represented a form of discrimination against LGBT students attending those schools. Biola University, a liberal arts college in Los Angeles, along with several other California Christian colleges and universities, argued that the bill, if passed, would not only violate their religious liberties but would prevent low-income students in need of financial aid from attending their institutions.[39]

The California bill had no bearing on federal funding or institutions outside California, but it still raised much fear among Christian colleges throughout the country. Liberty University students receive $445 million in federal student loans, the highest total of any four-year university in Virginia and the eighth-highest in the nation. (The high ranking in both categories is due, in part, to the sheer size of the Liberty student body.) As we saw in the case of Gordon College (in chapter 1), the Obama administration had been moving to limit federal funds to organizations that "discriminated" against the LGBT community. It may not be too much of an exaggeration to say that the future of Liberty University as the world's largest Christian university may have been in jeopardy had Hillary Clinton won the presidency in November 2016. With the Trump victory, Christian colleges are breathing a bit easier these days.[40]

Another religious-liberty issue that concerns many of the court evangelicals is the clause in the IRS tax code commonly referred to as the Johnson Amendment. The Johnson Amendment is a part of the code that forbids tax-exempt organizations such as churches from endorsing political candidates. Since 1954, when the Johnson Amendment was added to the code, only one church has ever lost its tax-exempt status for violating it.[41] Trump first learned about the amendment during some of his early meetings with evangelicals in Trump Tower. Since that time he has become fixated on it: he realized that the IRS would not allow evangelical pastors to endorse him or any other candidate without losing their tax-exempt status.[42] Trump promised his evangelical supporters that, if elected, he would bring an end to the Johnson Amendment.

For many evangelicals and their followers, Trump fulfilled that promise on May 4, 2017. In an outdoor ceremony at the White House, with court evangelicals and other religious leaders by his side, Donald Trump issued an executive order on religious liberty. Section 2 of the order included the statement: "In particular, the Secretary of the Treasury shall ensure, to the extent permitted by law, that the Department of the Treasury does not take any action against any individual, house of worship, or other religious organization on the basis that such individual or organization speaks or has spoken about moral or political issues from a religious perspective." The statement was a reference to the Johnson Amendment without explicitly naming it. After he signed the order, Trump told the faith leaders present: "You're now in a position to say what you want to say . . . no one should be censoring sermons or targeting pastors."[43]

Court evangelicals cheered the new order, but in reality it did absolutely nothing to change the Johnson Amendment. The order was little more than a symbolic gesture meant to appease evangelicals and keep their support. What may have been a public relations victory for Trump and the court evangelicals did not amount to anything because the president does not have the authority to change the tax code—that job belongs to Congress.[44] And when Congress did overhaul the tax code in December 2017, the Johnson Amendment was not removed.

But the attempts to repeal the Johnson Amendment exposed something deeper: a serious flaw in the way that many conservative evangelicals think about the relationship between church and state. According to a 2012 poll, eighty-six percent of evangelical pastors believed that clergy should not endorse political candidates from the pulpit.[45] Those who do want to endorse candidates from the pulpit, and have turned the Johnson Amendment into a political issue, seem more concerned about freedom of speech than they are about the way this kind of political partisanship undermines their gospel witness. There is an old Baptist saying about religion and politics that goes something like this: "If you mix horse manure and ice cream, it doesn't do much to the manure, but it sure does ruin the ice cream." When the government starts telling evangelical pastors what they can and cannot preach in terms of theology, biblical interpretation, or ethics (even sexual ethics), we have a problem; but the Johnson Amendment is not this kind of problem. Evangelicals should be thankful for the Johnson Amendment: it is a useful reminder from an unlikely source about the spiritual dangers that arise when sanctuaries are used as campaign offices.

The third major issue championed by the court evangelicals is the United States recognition of Jerusalem as the "eternal capital" of the Jewish people. The government could accomplish this by moving its embassy from Tel Aviv to Jerusalem. Ted Cruz made this a major campaign promise during the GOP primaries, but it was Donald Trump who delivered for conservative evangelicals on December 4, 2017. One of the reasons conservative evangelicals are ecstatic about this move is that many of them believe, as we saw in chapter 3, that biblical prophecy teaches that the return of the Jews to Israel is a prerequisite for the Second Coming of Jesus Christ. Christ will one day return to earth with his raptured saints and descend on a rebuilt temple located inside Jerusalem. Robert Jeffress is one of the most outspoken defenders of Trump's decision to move the capital to the holy city. He has written several books on biblical prophecy and is a graduate of Dallas Theological Seminary, the center of Dispensational theology in America. Jeffress told Fox News that Trump is now "on the right side of history" and on the "right side of God."[46]

Trump's decision to move the embassy, which no doubt came after much lobbying from the court evangelicals, is not only a triumph for the Dispensationalists; it also fits well with INC apostle Lance Wallnau's prophecy that Donald Trump is a new King Cyrus. This merger of Dispensational theology and INC prophecy appears in court evangelical Mike Evans's response to Trump's move. One of America's leading Christian Zionists, Evans recently founded the Friends of Zion Heritage Center and the Friends of Zion Museum in Jerusalem to celebrate the "everlasting bond between the Jewish and Christian peoples." When Trump announced that he was moving the American embassy to Jerusalem, Evans enthusiastically told the Christian Broadcasting Network that when he next saw Trump in the Oval Office he would say to him: "Cyrus, you're Cyrus. Because you've done something historic and prophetic." Wallnau envisioned Trump as a Cyrus who would save American Christians; Evans believed that Trump was a modern-day Cyrus who would make possible the restoration of Jerusalem and the further confirmation of Israel's future role in biblical prophecy. Because of Trump's actions, Evans declared, the blessing of God would come upon America. Indeed, this decision would make America great in the eyes of God.[47] It also made Trump great in the eyes of the court evangelicals, raising questions about whether his decision to move the American embassy to Jerusalem was more of a political move than a diplomatic or religious one.

Playing with Politics, Getting Burned

Billy Graham was the official spokesperson for American evangelicalism for more than five decades. Historian Grant Wacker has described him as "America's Pastor." He was also the first court evangelical, until he learned the hard way— and far too late—about the seductions of that power. Graham prayed at the presidential inaugurations of Richard Nixon, George H. W. Bush, and Bill Clinton and was involved in other religious events at the inaugurations of Lyndon Johnson, Ronald Reagan, and George W. Bush. He developed a friendship with every American president from Harry S. Truman to Barack Obama. Graham mostly served as spiritual counselor to the man in the Oval Office, but his status as one of the most popular and beloved figures in the world also meant that presidents and presidential candidates coveted his endorsement during election seasons.

Graham was a strong anticommunist and remained fascinated with politics his entire life, so much so that he did not shy away from offering political advice. Graham attacked Truman for failing to escalate the Korean War. He supported Dwight Eisenhower because he believed that Ike would end communism. Eisenhower, for his part, was happy to tell the nation that Graham was a Republican. In 1960, harboring doubts about John F. Kennedy because of his Catholicism,

Graham appeared on the campaign trail with Richard Nixon and came very close to formally endorsing him. Nixon and Graham had established a correspondence in 1955, and as historian Steven P. Miller describes them, Graham's letters reflect "the flattery he routinely lobbed at political authorities of all stripes." In one letter, Graham describes Nixon as the "greatest Vice President in history." In another he suggests that biblical prophecy might help Eisenhower make sense of his Middle East policy. Nixon hoped that Graham would help him win the South in 1960, and he often turned to the latter for political advice.[48]

Graham's relationship with Richard Nixon brought him closer to the world of presidential politics than he had ever been before. The two stayed in close contact during the years following Nixon's loss to Kennedy in the election of 1960, and the evangelist continued to speak positively about the politician in public venues. In a 1964 interview in *McCall's* magazine, Graham expressed his bafflement that he often heard people say "I just don't like Nixon." According to Graham, the former vice president was "one of the warmest and most likable men I have ever known." Nixon claimed that Graham encouraged him to run for president again in 1968, and Graham, in turn, suggested that Nixon's second chance at the nation's highest political office was part of God's providential plan. During Nixon's years in the White House (1969–1974), Graham made regular visits to the president, served as an unofficial surrogate (without formally endorsing him), advised Nixon on policy decisions, and publicly thanked God for his presidency. Miller goes as far to suggest that there were times when "Graham's [religious] services or appearances seemed to double as Nixon rallies." Nixon used Graham to win evangelical votes, especially in the South, where Nixon needed the votes of white southern Christians—his so-called "Southern strategy"—and Graham believed that Nixon was a moral statesman, God's man to lead a Christian nation.[49]

But Graham would quickly learn that Richard Nixon was one man in Graham's presence and quite another when operating in the cutthroat world of presidential politics. During the Watergate scandal, Graham stood by the president. During the 1972 election campaign, he chided Nixon's opponent, South Dakota senator George McGovern, for saying that the Nixon administration was up to something sinister. In one letter to President Nixon, Graham quoted Psalm 35:11-12, where the psalmist writes: "They accuse me of things I have never heard about. I do them good, but they return me harm." Wacker says that Graham "continued to defend Nixon long after most Americans smelled a rat." In December 1973, the evangelist told Nixon that he had "complete confidence" in his "personal integrity." When transcripts of Nixon's Oval Office conversations (which included Nixon's strongly anti-Semitic language) proved that the president was ultimately responsible for the Watergate break-in, Graham seemed more concerned about Nixon's profanity on the tapes than the fact that the president was using his power to cover up his crimes. When Graham read excerpts of the tapes in *The New York Times*, he claimed to feel "physically sick." Years later, Graham admitted that his relationship with the disgraced former president had "muffled those inner monitors that had warned me for years to stay out of partisan politics" and, as Wacker notes, "he urged young evangelists to avoid his mistake."[50]

Graham may have eventually learned his lesson, but leaders of the next generation of conservative evangelicals did not. When Jerry Falwell Sr. founded the Moral Majority in 1979— in his attempt to clean up and win back America—journalist

Cal Thomas and evangelical pastor Ed Dobson were two of the Moral Majority's most important staff members. Thomas put his journalism career on hold to join Falwell in Lynchburg as the Moral Majority's vice president for communications. Dobson, a professor at Falwell's Liberty Baptist College (later to become Liberty University), served as a tireless promoter of the organization from his position as a member of the board. During the 1980s, those two were influential in shaping the direction of the Moral Majority. They believed in Falwell's vision completely and served the cause with passion and zeal.[51]

But in 1999, Dobson and Thomas reflected soberly on their experience with Falwell and the Moral Majority in their book *Blinded by Might: Can the Religious Right Save America?* They concluded that the answer to the subtitle's question was a definitive "no." Neither Dobson nor Thomas left evangelicalism or ceased their commitment to conservative causes; but they were forced to admit that the political strategy they helped to forge in the 1980s had failed. Despite their efforts, *Roe v. Wade* had not been overturned. The Internet had made pornography more accessible than ever. Drug use had not subsided, and crime had not dissipated in any significant way. In the process, the prophetic witness of the evangelical church was subordinated to political power and all its trappings. As Cal Thomas put it, in a reference to Palm Sunday, "Who wanted to ride into the capital on the back of an ass when one could go first class in a private jet and be picked up and driven around in a chauffeured limousine?"[52]

Thomas, who parlayed his Moral Majority fame into a nationally syndicated newspaper column, did not mince words when he disparaged the evangelical pursuit of political power. "Christian faith is about truth," he tells his readers, and "whenever you try to mix power and truth, power usually wins." Through his years with Falwell, Thomas learned how power is the "ultimate aphrodisiac." It is not only seductive, but also affects the judgment of the one who "takes it." Thomas warned his evangelical readers how the chase for political power threatens the spread of the gospel. He quoted the late Catholic priest Henri Nouwen: "The temptation to consider power an apt instrument for the proclamation of the gospel is the greatest temptation of all." Thomas pointed to the myriad ways in which the Moral Majority—and the Christian Right agenda that it spawned—played to the fears of white evangelicals. For example, Moral Majority fundraising letters always followed a basic formula: "First, they identify an enemy: homosexuals, abortionists, Democrats, or 'liberals' in general. Second, the enemies are accused of being out to 'get us' or to impose their morality on the rest of the country. Third, the letter assures the reader that something will be done. . . . Fourth, to get this job done, please send money." Thomas completely rejected the court evangelical notion that Christians need to have a "seat at the table." "Access" to political power, he argued, required compromise of "cherished and deeply held convictions." He added: "Religious leaders who seek favor with the king run the risk of refusing to speak truth to power out of fear that they won't be invited back." Thomas and Dobson offer a cautionary tale to today's court evangelicals based on their own extensive experience in the king's court.[53]

Thomas and Dobson were not the only ones burned. David Kuo, a young evangelical political operative and speechwriter, was a conservative, pro-life, born-again Christian with a passionate desire—born out of what he believed his faith required of him—to serve the poor with compassion. He was convinced that government had a role to play in this process, and it led him to pursue a career in Washington. Kuo wrote speeches for prominent GOP political leaders such as Jack Kemp, Bill Bennett, John Ashcroft, Ralph Reed, Dan Quayle, and George W. Bush. He eventually found himself in the latter Bush's White House, where he served in the president's newly formed Office of Faith-Based and Neighborhood Partnerships. Bush had established that office by an executive order shortly after he took office in January 2001. It was part of his commitment to what he and others were describing as "compassionate conservatism," an approach to conservative politics that focused on addressing issues such as immigration, poverty, and health care via a mixture of government programs, religious organizations, charities, and private interests. Kuo believed that compassionate conservatism offered him a way of blending his evangelical faith with his political activism.[54]

Very early in his tenure at the White House, Kuo realized that political power and Christian compassion do not mix very well. His efforts in the Office of Faith-Based and Neighborhood Partnerships were largely ignored unless they were an immediate benefit to Bush's political fortunes. Most of the White House staff simply ignored Kuo's work. Republican congressmen did not care as much about compassion as they did about tax cuts, economic growth, and a strong military. In the 2004 presidential election, a contest in which evangelicals played a major role in Bush's victory over John Kerry, Kuo did some soul-searching. Was he engaged in politics as a means of serving God and helping those in need, or was he using his role in the Office of Faith-Based and Neighborhood Partnerships to win votes for Bush? "There is an enormous difference between the two possibilities," he wrote. "One sought to serve Jesus' concerns for people through political ends. The other sought to serve a political end by using Jesus' concerns as justification."[55]

In his book *Tempted by Faith*, Kuo describes a Bush administration, led by the president's top political adviser, Karl Rove, that gave lip service—and little more—to matters important to the Christian community. He watched as the Bush White House did whatever they could to keep faith leaders happy. They invited evangelicals to events and meetings, called them on the phone, offered them tickets to be part of the crowd when Air Force One landed in their towns, and gave them "little trinkets like cufflinks or pens or pads of paper" that they could take home and show their followers "just how influential they were." Kuo was brutally honest: "Making politically active Christians personally happy meant having to worry far less about the Christian political agenda." He even began to question whether Bush himself cared about the compassionate agenda that helped him win the presidency. Kuo had known Bush since his days as governor of Texas, and he truly believed that the president's heart was in the right place; but then he was disappointed at how little the president did to carry that agenda forward. Kuo leaves his readers with some sobering thoughts about the relationship between religion and politics:

> For . . . the White House staff, evangelical leaders were people to be tolerated, not people who were truly welcomed. No group was more eye-rolling about Christians than the political affairs shop. They knew "the nuts" were politically invaluable, but that was the extent of their usefulness. Sadly, the political affairs folks complained most often and most loudly about how boorish many politically involved Christians were. They didn't see much of the love of Jesus in their lives. . . . There wasn't a week that went by that I didn't hear someone in the middle-to-senior levels making

some comment or another about how annoying the Christians were or how tiresome they were, or how "handling" them took so much time. National Christian leaders received hugs and smiles in person and then were dismissed behind their backs and described as "ridiculous," "out of control," and just plain "goofy."

David Kuo, who died of a brain tumor in 2013, realized that the White House is "one of the most seductive places imaginable. Not just because of the perks . . . but because of the raw power of the place hidden in true desire to save the world."[56]

CHAPTER 5

MAKE AMERICA
GREAT AGAIN

Together, we will make America strong again. We will make
America wealthy again. We will make America proud again.
We will make America safe again. And yes, together we will
make America great again. Thank you. God bless you. And
God bless America.

— Donald Trump,
Inauguration Address, January 20, 2017

I n early 2013, I received an email from Rev. Ray McMillan,
the pastor of Faith Christian Center, a conservative evangelical and largely African American congregation in Cincinnati, Ohio. McMillan was writing to ask me if I might be
interested in participating on a panel at an upcoming conference on evangelicals and racial reconciliation, to be held
later that year at Wheaton College, a Christian liberal arts college in western suburban Chicago. I was initially surprised
by the invitation. I cared about racial reconciliation, but I
had never spoken at a conference on the subject. I was not an

expert in the field, and even my own historical work did not dive explicitly into race or the history of people of color in the United States. I was even more confused when Rev. McMillan asked me to be part of a plenary presentation on the subject of my recent book, *Was America Founded as a Christian Nation?* I thought I could probably say a few things about race and the American founding, but I also wondered if someone more prepared, and perhaps more of an activist in this area, might be better suited to speak in my time slot. After a follow-up phone conversation with Rev. McMillan, I began to see what he was up to. He told me that he and other Cincinnati pastors were noticing a disturbing trend in their African American and interracial congregations. Many of their parishioners had accepted the idea, propagated by the Christian Right, that the United States was founded as a Christian nation. McMillan believed that such an understanding of history was troubling for African American evangelicals. The promoters of this view were convincing many African Americans in Cincinnati that they needed to "reclaim" or "restore" America to its supposedly Christian roots in order to win the favor of God. McMillan could not stomach the idea that a country that was committed to slavery, Jim Crow laws, and all kinds of other racial inequalities could ever call itself "Christian." Why would any African American want to "reclaim" a history steeped in racism? If America was indeed built on Judeo-Christian principles, then its Founders would one day stand before God and explain why they did not apply these beliefs to African Americans. And if America was not founded as a Christian nation, McMillan needed to tell his congregation that they had been sold a bill of goods.

I often think about Rev. McMillan and the Wheaton conference on racial reconciliation whenever Donald Trump says that he wants to "make America great again." I assume that most people, when they hear this phrase, focus on the word "great." But as a historian, I am much more interested in Trump's use of the word "again." For white Americans, "making America great again" invokes nostalgia for days gone by. America was great when the economy was booming, or when the culture was less coarse, or when the nuclear family looked like the Cleaver family on *Leave It to Beaver,* or when public-school children prayed and read the Bible at the start of each day. But as I listened to the African American ministers at the Wheaton conference, I came face to face with the reality that African Americans have very little to be nostalgic about. As one of those preachers observed, "The best time to be black in the United States is right now!" When African Americans look back, they see the oppression of slavery, the burning crosses, the lynched bodies, the poll taxes and literacy tests, the separate but unequal schools, the "colored-only" water fountains, and the backs of buses. Make America great again?

Christian America?

When many conservative evangelical supporters of Donald Trump first heard the phrase "make America great again," they probably assumed that America *was* indeed great until the Supreme Court, through a series of cases, removed God from public life. If America was founded as a "shining city on a hill" and continued to exist in a unique, exclusive, and exceptional covenant relationship with God long after the decline of Puritanism, then the Christian Right might have a legitimate case. But if America was not founded as a Christian nation, the entire foundation of their political agenda collapses.

Christians would still be justified in fighting against abortion and gay marriage, or advocating for religious liberty; but it would be a lot more difficult to use American history to make their case.

As I argued in *Was America Founded as a Christian Nation?*, until the 1970s, Americans—evangelicals and non-evangelicals alike— believed that they were living in a Christian nation. This is merely a historical statement. I do not mean to suggest that such a view was right or wrong. Neither is it a statement about whether those who made this claim interpreted the Founding Fathers correctly on the matter. To ask whether America was founded as a Christian nation is to take a debate that did not reach any degree of intensity until recently and to superimpose it on an eighteenth-century world of the white men who built the American republic. The Founding Fathers lived in a world that was fundamentally different from our own. It was a world in which Christianity was the only game in town. To be sure, there were some small Jewish communities located in coastal cities, and it is likely that a form of Islam may have been practiced among some African slaves. But the powerful influence of Christianity, especially Protestant Christianity, held unrivaled influence.

The Founding Fathers also had very divergent views of the relationship between Christianity and the nation they were forging. We need to stop treating them as a monolithic whole. Thomas Jefferson and James Madison, for example, were strong advocates for the complete separation of church and state. John Adams and George Washington, like their fellow Federalists whom we met in chapter 3, believed that religion was essential to the cultivation of a virtuous citizenry. It is true that the Founders, by virtue of the fact that they signed the Declaration of Independence, probably believed in a God who presided over nature, was the author of human rights, would one day judge the dead, and who governed the world by his providence. Those who signed the US Constitution endorsed the idea that there should be no religious test— Christian or otherwise—required of those wishing to hold federal office. Those responsible for the First Amendment also championed the free exercise of religion and rejected a state-sponsored church.

Yet anyone who wants to use these documents to argue against the importance of religion—in the America of the time of the founding—must reckon with early state constitutions, such as those in Pennsylvania, Massachusetts, and South Carolina, that required officeholders to affirm the inspiration of the Old and New Testaments, to obey the Christian Sabbath, or to contribute tax money to support a state church. Some of the Founders believed that Christians, and only Christians, should be running their state governments. Other Founders rejected the idea of the separation of church and state. Virginia, for example, banned all test oaths and religious establishments. And so, was America founded as a Christian nation? A close examination of the American past makes it very difficult to answer with a definitive "yes" or "no."[1]

This leads us to a second question: Is America a Christian nation today? It all depends on what one means by "Christian nation." In terms of the religious affiliation of its population, the United States is unquestionably a Christian nation—in the sense that most Americans identify with some form of the Christian faith. As I noted above, while Christianity has had a defining influence on American culture, that influence has waned dramatically in the last fifty years. Moreover, from a legal and constitutional standpoint, it is impossible to suggest that the United States is now a Christian nation. Article 6 of the US Constitution still forbids religious tests for office. The First Amendment still does not allow a religious establishment and still secures religious freedom for all Americans. The fact that the individual states at the time of the founding upheld test oaths or supported state churches became irrelevant to this conversation when the Supreme Court, in *Everson v. Board* (1947), applied the due-process clause of the Fourteenth Amendment to the establishment clause of the First Amendment. In other words, the Supreme Court made it clear that states now had to abide by the US Constitution and the Bill of Rights in matters of religion much in the same way that states no longer had the right to make their own decisions about whether slavery was legal. Many white evangelicals, especially those who champion the rights of states to chart their own course on matters pertaining to religion and political life, are not happy about what the court did in *Everson*. But it remains the law of the land.

It is easy for white evangelicals to look back fondly on American history. There is, of course, a lot to celebrate. We are a nation founded on the belief that human beings are "endowed by our Creator with certain inalienable rights, namely, life, liberty, and the pursuit of happiness." We have established some of the greatest colleges and universities in the world. Our standard of living exceeds those in other countries. When we have failed to live up to our ideas we have made efforts to correct our moral indiscretions. Those who fought tirelessly to end slavery, curb the negative effects of alcohol, defend human life, and deliver rights to women and the less fortunate come to mind. Americans have proven that they can act with a sense of common purpose and unity. We have seen the American character on display, for example, during two World Wars and in the wake of the September 11, 2001, terrorist attacks. And the United States has always been a place where immigrants can come and start new lives.

At the same time, America is a nation that has been steeped in racism, xenophobia, imperialism, violence, materialism, and a host of other practices that do not conform very well to the ethical demands that Christianity places upon our lives. Christians should be very careful when they long for the days when America was apparently "great." Too many conservative evangelicals view the past through the lens of nostalgia. Scholar Svetlana Boym describes nostalgia as a "sentiment of loss and displacement" that "inevitably reappears as a defense mechanism in a time of accelerated rhythms of life and historical upheavals."[2] In this sense, nostalgia is closely related to fear. In times of great social and cultural change, the nostalgic person will turn to a real or an imagined past as an island of safety amid the raging storms of progress. In other words, to quote Boym again, "progress didn't cure nostalgia but exacerbated it." Sometimes evangelicals will seek refuge from change in a Christian past that never existed in the first place. At other times they will try to travel back to a Christian past that did exist—but, like the present, was compromised by sin.

Nostalgia is thus a powerful political tool. A politician who claims to have the power to take people back to a time when America was great stands a good chance of winning the votes of fearful men and women. In the end, the practice of nostalgia is inherently selfish because it focuses entirely on our own experience of the past and not on the experience of others. For example, people nostalgic for the world of *Leave It to Beaver* may fail to recognize that other people, perhaps even some of the people living in the Cleaver's suburban "paradise" of the 1950s, were not experiencing the world in a way that they would describe as "great." Nostalgia can give us tunnel vision. Its selective use of the past fails to recognize the complexity and breadth of the human experience—the good and the bad of American history, the eras that we want to (re)experience (if only for a moment) and those we do not. Conservative evangelicals who sing the praises of America's "Judeo-Christian heritage" today, and those who yearn for a Christian golden age, are really talking about the present rather than the past.

Take, for example, the Christian nationalism of one of Trump's most prominent court evangelicals, Robert Jeffress of the First Baptist Church in Dallas. For the past several years Jeffress has been preaching a sermon to his congregation and radio audience entitled "America Is a Christian Nation." Jeffress begins his sermon in the present by calling attention to his belief that "our government is ceasing to acknowledge any kind of acknowledgment of God . . . in the public square." He then rattles off a list of examples, from towns prohibiting prayers at high school football games to the banning of nativity scenes in public spaces. Jeffress does not stop there: "We are told repeatedly that our country's founders were secularists, deists, sprinkled with a few Christians who came to this nation seeking above all other things to build an un-scalable wall between the government and Christianity. And most importantly, they wanted to compartmentalize Christianity to the state and the home." With the present problem diagnosed, Jeffress then attempts to marshal the past as way of solving these problems: "I realize it is [politically] incorrect to say this, but it is nevertheless true. America was not founded as a Muslim nation. America was not founded as a Hindu nation. America was not founded as a nation that is neutral toward Christianity. America was founded as a Christian nation, and today we are going to discover that truth from history."[3]

One problematic historical reference after another fill the remainder of Jeffress's sermon. He makes the wildly exaggerated claim that fifty-two of the original fifty-five signers of the Constitution were "evangelical believers." He peddles the false notion that the disestablishment clause in the First Amendment was meant to apply solely to Protestant denominations, meaning that the founders did not want a "Presbyterian nation" or a "Baptist nation," but simply assumed that we were a Christian nation. There is no evidence in the writings of the Founders to support this interpretation, although, as Jeffress notes, there were some nineteenth-century Supreme Court justices who interpreted the disestablishment clause this way. Based on this argument, he concludes that "we do not restrict other people's right to worship however they choose to worship, but that doesn't mean we treat all religions equally. This is a Christian nation! Every other religion is an imposter, an infidel." Jeffress also declares that the test oaths and Christian establishments in the earliest state constitutions still apply today, and he misinterprets the 1892 *Church of the Holy Trinity v. United States* case as a definitive statement that the United States was a Christian nation, when in fact that case was simply about immigration. Near the end of his sermon, Jeffress throws in his assumption that spikes in violence, illegitimate births, divorce, and low SAT scores in America are the direct product of the Supreme Court's decision to remove prayer and Bible-reading from public schools.[4]

I do not have the space in the book to counter in depth the false and problematic claims Jeffress makes in his "America Is a Christian Nation" sermon. But it is worth noting that his manipulation of the past to advance his Christian Right agenda and scare his congregation into political action comes straight out of the playbook of David Barton, his friend and fellow conservative political activist. (Jeffress mentions a recent Barton visit to First Baptist-Dallas in the sermon). Nearly everything Jeffress says in this sermon he lifted from Barton's Wallbuilders website. For the past thirty years, Barton, a GOP operative from Aledo, Texas, has provided pastors and conservative politicians with inaccurate or misinterpreted facts used to fuel the Christian Right's politics of nostalgia. Barton's understanding of the past has been debunked by nearly every serious American historian, including those who teach at the most conservative Christian colleges; but he continues to maintain a large following in the evangelical community. Barton is not a historian; he is a politician who uses the past to achieve the political goals of restoring America to its supposedly Christian roots. (In fact, Barton was one of the authors that Rev. Ray McMillan mentioned when he invited me to the Wheaton College conference to help set the record straight.) Barton has strong ties to the court evangelicals. He ran a Ted Cruz super-PAC during the 2016 GOP primary season, and when Cruz dropped out of the race, he threw his support behind Donald Trump. As far as I can tell, Barton never called Trump a modern-day Cyrus, but he did declare Trump to be "God's guy" and has on multiple occasions claimed that his work in bringing his Christian views of the past to bear on government is part of the "Seven Mountains of Influence" strategy popular among the INC prophets we met in the preceding chapter.[5]

The Christian nationalism of Robert Jeffress, David Barton, the court evangelicals, and many of their followers cannot be ignored when one seeks to explain the 81 percent of white evangelical voters who voted for Trump. Not all white conservative evangelicals are that interested in history, but they do believe at some level that the United States was founded as, and continues to be, a Christian nation. If they don't get this from David Barton, they certainly pick it up from Fox News and conservative talk radio. The relationship between religion and the founding of the United States is a complicated topic, but saying "it's complicated" does not win voters or feed the culture wars. For many conservative evangelicals, the past is only useful when it is carefully packaged to appeal to the fear and nostalgia of evangelicals worried about the moral collapse of their nation and the possibility that God might turn his back on America. Social decline is only possible when understood in relation to a previous utopia. America can only be made great *again* if it was great at some point in history.

While the Barton view of American history is both inaccurate and conducive to the kind of Christian political agenda that led evangelicals to vote for Trump; it is also problematic in a theological sense. The belief that the United States is a Christian nation is a form of idolatry.[6] First, it is worth remembering that God performs his redemptive work through individuals, not nations. If this is true, then a Christian nation is impossible. As political theorist Glenn Tinder puts it: "Society cannot be formed in accordance with sacred norms . . . as some Christians have desired, and if the attempt to do so is made, the result will be less a sacralization of society than a degradation of the sacred." The United States is not the kingdom of God, and it never will be. Tinder continues:

> The Church is an implicit condemnation of national pride, and there are no more shameful chapters in Christian history than those that show churchmen uncritically, sometimes fanatically, endorsing the ambitions and moral arrogance of their national governments. To ask nations to forswear national pride—the pride of uninhibited selfishness . . . may be asking too

much. But to ask the Church openly to oppose such pride does not seem extreme.

As Christians, we live in a society with rules and laws necessary to maintain order in a broken world. But in the end, society is sinful, power will usually corrupt, and government, while indispensable, will always be "deceptive, selfish, arrogant—and often atrocious." We are constantly in jeopardy of making idols out of political leaders by placing our sacred hopes in them. Meanwhile, we remain deaf and blind to a Christian tradition that teaches us to place our hope in the resurrection of the dead and the life of the world to come. We contribute to this world in the ways that God has called us to contribute to it. We work for peace and justice when violence and oppression rear their ugly heads. We remain attentive to God through Scripture, prayer, and the rest of the spiritual disciplines. And we wait for the day when God's kingdom will be revealed in all its fullness.[7] Meanwhile, we already have a Strongman in our corner.

When Robert Jeffress claims that we should not treat all religions equally, and that non-Christian religions are imposters and infidels, he conflates the church and the state. Though his language is harsh, lacking in charity, and completely void of humility, Jeffress is correct when he says that evangelicals believe that the adherents of other religions are in error. But these are arguments that we have in church, not in the public square. Because Christian nationalists, based on their sketchy view of history, believe that Christianity should be a privileged religion, they are left unable to articulate a vision of pluralism. Most conservative evangelicals would embrace the view that all men and women have human dignity because they have been created in the image of God. They would also say that God is a God of liberty. If these assumptions are true, then one cannot embrace the kind of Christian nation that Jeffress defends so vigorously. In a nation of liberty, the government does not interfere with how people use their freedom to make choices for or against religion. Once again, Glenn Tinder is helpful here:

> When Christians accept liberty they accept the possibility—a possibility that is almost certain to become a reality—of a world unformed by and ungoverned by faith. . . . The natural inclination of faith is to build a sacred order—to reconstruct the world in its own image. In granting liberty, it abandons that spontaneous project. It acquiesces in secularism—life unrelated to God and unstructured by faith. Acknowledging the right of human beings to be free, it allows for a repudiation of faith. . . . Granting liberty is making way for sin. . . . When Christians commit themselves to liberty there follows an enormous complication of Christian morality; they deliberately refrain, in some measure, from resisting evil. They allow the tares to grow with the wheat.[8]

Trump and American History

It is doubtful that Donald Trump knows or cares much about the debate over whether the United States is a Christian nation. He likes to talk about the Johnson Amendment, religious liberty, and the idea that Americans "worship God, not government," but he seldom refers to America as a Christian nation. This makes him different from Ted Cruz, Marco Rubio, Mike

Huckabee, Ben Carson, Bobby Jindal, and Rick Santorum—
all candidates who made this belief a central theme in their
2016 campaigns. While I am sure Trump would be happy to
declare that America is a Christian nation should the court
evangelicals push him in that direction, his use of the phrase
"make America great again" transcends the concerns of his
evangelical base.

We now return to the question of exactly when Donald
Trump thinks America was great. Was it during the time of the
American Revolution? The Gilded Age? The Industrial Revolution? The 1920s? The 1950s? The Reagan Era? If we can nail down
the era or eras when America was "great," perhaps we can
begin to make progress on the question of whether Trump's
campaign slogan has any merit. Since he has never been completely clear or specific about which moments in American
history were great—though I think it's fair to say that we can
eliminate the Civil War and the Great Depression—we must
rely on the periods and personalities of yesteryear that Trump
has evoked most often, both on the campaign trail and in his
first year in office. Anyone who has watched and listened to
Trump closely knows that he has a special affinity for the character of Andrew Jackson, the phrases "America first" and "law
and order," and an immigration policy that he says is modeled
on something called "Operation Wetback." What is striking
about his use of these historical references is the fact that all of
them, in one way or another, have to do with race relations in
America. Considering Trump's difficulties in condemning the
white supremacists in Charlottesville, his claim that a judge
would not give him, an Anglo, a fair trial because the judge was
Hispanic, and his participation in the Barack Obama "birther"
controversy, it is difficult not to see his use of the past in this
context.

Donald Trump did not find Andrew Jackson; Andrew Jackson found him. When historians and pundits began to compare Trump the populist with Jackson the populist, the candidate took notice. Moreover, Jackson is a favorite of Steve Bannon, Trump's former political adviser and campaign manager. By the time Trump entered the White House in late January 2017, an 1835 Ralph E. W. Earle portrait of Andrew Jackson was hanging in the Oval Office. In March 2017, Trump visited Jackson's home in Nashville and laid a wreath on his tomb to commemorate the seventh president's 250th birthday. There was also, of course, Trump's misinformed claim about Jackson and the Civil War:

> I mean, had Andrew Jackson been a little later, you wouldn't have had the Civil War. He was a very tough person, but he had a big heart. He was really angry that he saw what was happening with regard to the Civil War, he said "There is no reason for this." People don't realize, you know the Civil War, if you think about it, why? People don't ask that question, but why was there a Civil War? Why could that one not have been worked out?[9]

Historians were quick to jump on the president's comments by pointing out that the overwhelming consensus is that the Civil War was fought over slavery. Andrew Jackson owned a hundred slaves and had always been a strong advocate for the spread of that institution into the West of this country. Jackson died in 1845; the Civil War began in 1861. And if Jackson had been around to do something about the tensions between North and South, he would have probably sympathized with the Confederacy.[10]

Andrew Jackson was president of the United States during what historians call the "Age of Democracy." Universal manhood suffrage (the right for white men to vote regardless of how much property they owned), the rise of something akin to the modern political parties, and the influx of millions of new immigrants, changed American politics forever. Democracy in that era empowered white men. While nothing close to social equality emerged then, political participation did reach an all-time high. Jackson's life story, which was characterized by a rise from poverty and hardship, made him the ideal man to lead the country in this new democratic age. His popularity among ordinary voters was unprecedented. By the time he entered office in 1829, Jackson had risen above the hardships of his past, had a national reputation as an Indian fighter and slaveowner, and was well known as the hero of the Battle of New Orleans, the last battle of the War of 1812. Jackson was a man of passion who often let his temper get the best of him. His lack of self-control prompted the elderly Thomas Jefferson to wonder whether Jackson's emotional volatility might disqualify him from the presidency.

Jackson won 56 percent of the vote in the 1828 presidential election and, as a result, believed he had a mandate to serve the people who cast ballots on his behalf. Jackson viewed himself as a savior of the ordinary farmers and workers who voted for him by the millions, and his commitment to these men shaped his policy decisions, especially when he dealt with the elites who controlled American financial institutions such as the National Bank. Jackson was a strong nationalist: during the nullification crisis, he turned against South Carolina, a state filled with fellow slaveholders, because he did not believe that a single state had the right to reject any law (in the case of South Carolina it was a tariff law) over the sovereign will

168

of the American people as represented in the Union. When the passion-filled Jackson asked Congress to pass a "force bill" enabling him to use the army to crush dissent in the Palmetto state, talk of civil war was in the air. In the end cooler heads prevailed and Congress reached a compromise to avoid secession and military conflict. Jackson's show of force further solidified his support among the nation's working people.

During his speech at Jackson's tomb, Donald Trump described the former president as a "product of his times." This was especially true when it came to race, slavery, and Jackson's policy toward Native Americans. Much of Jackson's Southern constituency relied on the president to defend slavery and white supremacy, and the president was more than happy to oblige. As we saw in chapter 3, many of these slaveholders lived in fear of insurrections. Poor whites who did not own slaves worried about what might happen to them if slaves were set free and forced to integrate into white society. For example, in 1835, during his second term as president, Jackson, in a blatant attempt to limit free speech, tried to stop the United States Post Office from delivering abolitionist literature into the South. "Democracy" was white.

When it came to Native Americans, Jackson believed that they were racially inferior and an impediment to the advancement of white settlement across the continent. He eventually developed what he described as a "just, humane, liberal policy toward the Indians" that would remove them from their lands to unoccupied territory west of the Mississippi. He believed that he was a great father to the Indians. He explained his decision to oust them from their ancestral lands by claiming that he was protecting them from a possible race war with whites drunk on Manifest Destiny. Drunk or not, the white men who voted for him in 1828 and 1832 simply wanted the Indians out of the way. Jackson, as a steward of the people who supported him in a democratic election, needed to act in response to their will. During the 1830s, Cherokee, Creek, Choctaw, Chickasaw, and Seminole Indians from Georgia, Alabama, Mississippi, and Florida, escorted by the United States Army, embarked on what has been described as the "Trail of Tears." Thousands of natives made the 800-mile trek to Jackson's new "Indian Territory," located in what is Oklahoma today.

It is fair to call Andrew Jackson a populist president. By the time he took office, he was a wealthy man, but he always presented himself as one of the people, a defender of the "humble members of society—the farmers, mechanics, and laborers." Yet, as we have seen, Jackson's nationalism, populism, and commitment to democracy was deeply charged with racial hatred and the defense of white supremacy. Is this the era of American history that Donald Trump has in mind when he says he wants to make America great *again*?

Or perhaps Trump means the era of "America First." In both his campaign and the initial year of his presidency, Trump reminded his base that they could expect him to always "put America first." Thus far, the phrase has been applied to foreign policy initiatives based on American nationalism. In April 2016, Trump announced that "my foreign policy will always put the interests of the American people and American security above all else. . . . That will be the foundation of every single decision that I will make. 'America First' will be the major and overriding theme of my administration." Trump's plan links economic prosperity on the domestic front with American influence overseas, but it has also played out in his decision to withdraw the United States from the Paris Climate Agreement and the Trans-Pacific Partnership, his plan to build a wall on the United States border with Mexico to protect the interests of American citizens from illegal immigrants, and his travel ban on Muslims entering the country. "America first" was a major theme of his inaugural address on January 20, 2017.[11]

For historians, the use of this phrase has echoes of the America First Committee, a student organization begun at Yale University in 1940 (future president Gerald R. Ford was a member), which petitioned the United States to stay out of World War II and to try, instead, to negotiate a peace settlement with Adolf Hitler. The group eventually included CEOs of major corporations (including Sears-Roebuck and the *Chicago Tribune*), members of Congress, and hundreds of local chapters around the country. In 1941, Charles Lindbergh, who was internationally known for piloting the first solo transatlantic flight in 1927, became the public face of the committee.

Soon the America First Committee became known for, more than anything else, its racism and anti-Semitism. Henry Ford, of Ford Motor Company fame, and Avery Brundage, the former chairman of the United States Olympic Committee, were removed from leadership positions because of their public anti-Semitism. Other committee members referred to President Franklin D. Roosevelt as "Jewish" and Winston Churchill as a "half-Jew." In September 1941, roughly three months before Pearl Harbor, Lindbergh told an audience in Des Moines, Iowa, that it was the Jews, "for reasons which are not American," who were trying to push the United States into World War II. Jews were a "foreign race" who controlled the entertainment industry and were in the process of infiltrating America's "political institutions." Commentators could not miss the connections between Lindbergh's isolationism and Hitler's concentration camps. One *New York Herald Tribune* columnist wrote: "I am absolutely certain that Lindbergh is pro-Nazi."[12]

BELIEVE ME

The America First Committee ended when the United States entered World War II, but the phrase has made a few brief appearances in recent American history. It was the slogan of conservative Pat Buchanan's 2000 Reform Party presidential campaign, a campaign that advocated for the United States to pull out of the World Trade Organization, the North American Free Trade Agreement, and to end US military intervention around the world. (Trump, who also competed for the Reform Party nomination in 2000, called Buchanan a "Hitler lover" and a candidate who appealed to the "really staunch-right wacko vote.") Today Trump says that he never thought about the way "America first" was used in the past and he does not really seem to care.[13] Yet one wonders: Is this what Donald Trump has in mind when he says he wants to make America great *again*?

During much of his 2016 presidential campaign, Donald Trump's immigration policy was simple: he would build a wall; Mexico would pay for it; and this wall would prevent drug-dealers, gang members, rapists, and other assorted illegal immigrants from coming into the country and harming honest, hard-working (majority-white) Americans. By the time he had secured the GOP nomination in the spring of 2016, he had perfected the politics of fear. In November 2015, Trump announced that, if he were to be elected, he would organize a "deportation force" to remove eleven million illegal immigrants from the United States. He would model his strategy on "Operation Wetback," an Eisenhower-era plan that empowered border patrol agents to find undocumented immigrants—many of whom were engaged in agricultural work in the West—and send them back to Mexico on airplanes and banana boats. The name of Eisenhower's operation came from a racially charged term—"Wetback," which was used to describe Mexicans who

172

tried to come to America illegally by swimming across the Rio Grande River. Trump praised the success of Operation Wetback and made several efforts to connect it with the "nice" and "friendly" personality of Eisenhower.[14]

During the Great Depression, the United States deported nearly a half-million Mexican immigrants who were said to be taking jobs away from white Americans. But when World War II began, the need for farm labor increased. In 1942, the United States initiated its Bracero program: temporary manual laborers from Mexico were given free travel to the United States, were housed in labor camps, were provided with food and sanitation facilities, and were paid a minimum wage of thirty cents per hour. During World War II, the program recruited about 200,000 Mexican men. But the need for labor also prompted a rise in illegal immigration, since many growers preferred to hire undocumented workers instead of taking the time to go through the official channels that the Bracero program required. As the number of unauthorized immigrants grew, white Americans responded with their traditional fears about their safety and security. Others said that illegal immigrants were to blame for low wages in the agricultural sector. It was in response to this that the Eisenhower administration enacted Operation Wetback in June 1954.[15]

The US Immigration and Naturalization Service (INS), the organization that executed Operation Wetback, claimed that they arrested and deported over one million Mexican immigrants. About 750 immigrant officials accomplished this work. The government used aircraft to identify "wetbacks," and pilots radioed ground-crew jeeps, who then moved in for the arrests. Officials transported these people deep into the Mexican interior, often "dumping" them by the truckload into Mexican villages to minimize their chances of returning to the

United States. Critics of the operation complained that such a massive deportation created social problems in Mexico because thousands of unemployed laborers were wandering the streets. In fact, many died of sunstroke. Some INS administrators considered building a chainlink fence to prevent the undocumented workers from returning to the United States; but many in the state department feared that such a fence would be viewed by the Soviet Union as a sign of weakness.[16] Operation Wetback may have been considered a success by those who pushed for it, but plenty of Americans will remember it as another dark chapter in United States history. Is this an era of American history that Donald Trump has in mind when he says he wants to make America great *again*?

In the summer of 2016, in the wake of terrorist attacks, the fatal shootings of African American men in Louisiana and Minnesota and elsewhere by white police officers, and the killing of five police officers in Dallas, Trump spent a lot of his presidential campaign praising American law enforcement. In July he told a Virginia Beach audience that he was "the law and order candidate."[17] He also used that phrase at the Republican National Convention in Cleveland, a phrase that has often been used by those in authority when they want to quash public disorder. "In this race for the White House, I am the law and order candidate. . . . Our convention occurs at a time of crisis for our nation. The attacks on our police, and the terrorism in our cities, threaten our very way of life. Any politician who does not grasp this danger is not fit to lead our country."[18]

For most Americans, "law and order" is associated with Richard Nixon's 1968 presidential campaign. According to historian Michael Flamm, "law and order was the most important domestic issue in the presidential election and arguably the decisive factor in Richard Nixon's narrow triumph over Hubert Humphrey." As might be expected, the need to bring law and order to American streets was a response to a significant rise in crime during the 1960s, particularly among African Americans and juveniles in American cities. The high crime rate among black men brought fear to white working-class Americans. Flamm notes that "by the late 1960s, white Americans overwhelmingly associated street crime with African Americans, who were more than seventeen times likely as white men to be arrested for robbery."[19] The worst fears of white Americans materialized in the summer of 1967, when race riots broke out in Detroit and Newark. The violence continued in 1968 following the assassinations of Martin Luther King Jr. and Robert Kennedy. In Chicago, Mayor Richard Daley ordered his police officers to shoot looters on sight in the street. In Washington, DC, race riots, led by black activist Stokely Carmichael, came within blocks of the White House, prompting President Lyndon Johnson to dispatch federal troops armed with machine guns to quell the violence. Later in the year, the Chicago police used tear gas to control protesters at the Democratic National Convention.

The Nixon campaign capitalized on the chaos. Nixon promised that, if elected, he would end the riots—using force if necessary. His campaign blamed the lack of law and order on the Democrats and portrayed his opponent, Hubert Humphrey, as weak on crime. Nixon consistently denied that he used the phrase "law and order" to send a message to white voters who feared African American violence, but many of his conservative supporters clearly heard that message. Nixon walked a fine line on matters related to race. He was aware, from watching his independent opponent, George Wallace, that calling attention to racial difference worked very well in presidential campaigns, especially in the South. Yet Nixon was not Wallace: he opposed segregation and supported the Civil Rights Acts of 1964 and the Voting Rights Act of 1965. Still, when he was not in front of the cameras, he was not reticent about his disdain for the "damn negroes." He confided to his counsel, John Ehrlichman, that Lyndon Johnson's Great Society programs would not help African Americans because "blacks were genetically inferior to whites." After filming a campaign advertisement calling for law and order in public schools, Nixon said to his aides: "Yep, this hits it right on the nose . . . it's all about law and order and the damn Negro-Puerto Rican groups out there."[20]

Like Nixon, Donald Trump claims that his use of the term "law and order" has nothing to do with race. Yet when he combines the phrase with a steady drumbeat of attention to "Muslim terrorists" or illegal Mexican immigrants that he claims are committing violent crimes, he is sending a message to his largely white working-class constituency that he hears, shares, and prioritizes their fears. Trump wants to restore law and order to America much like Nixon promised to do in the 1960s. Is this what he has in mind when he says he wants to make America great *again*?

But the problem with Donald Trump's use of American history goes well beyond his desire to make America great again or his regular references to some of the darker moments in our past—moments that have tended to divide Americans rather than uniting them. His approach to history also reveals his narcissism. When Trump says that he doesn't care how "America first" was used in 1940s, or claims to be ignorant of Nixon's use of "law and order," he shows his inability to understand himself as part of a larger American story. As *Washington Post* columnist Michael Gerson wrote in the wake of Trump's pre-inauguration Twitter attack on civil rights icon John Lewis, a veteran of nonviolent marches who was severely beaten at Selma: "Trump seems to have no feel for, no interest in, the American story he is about to enter." Gerson describes Trump's behavior in this regard as the "essence of narcissism."[21] The columnist is right: Trump is incapable of seeing himself as part of a presidential history that is larger than himself. Not all presidents have been perfect, and others have certainly shown narcissistic tendencies; but most of them have been humbled by the office. Our best presidents thought about their four or eight years in power with historical continuity in mind. This required them to respect the integrity of the office and the unofficial moral qualifications that come with it. Trump, however, spits in the face of this kind of historical continuity. This isn't conservatism; it is progressive thinking at its worst. Alexis de Tocqueville once said, "Not only does democracy make men forget their ancestors, but also clouds their view of their descendants and isolates them from their contemporaries. Each man is forever thrown back on himself alone, and there is a danger that he may be shut up in the solitude of his own heart." Sam Wineburg, one of the country's foremost scholars of historical thinking, writes:

> For the narcissist sees the world—both the past and the present—in his own image. Mature historical understanding teaches us to do the opposite: to go beyond our own image, to go beyond our brief life, and to go beyond the fleeting moment in human history into which we are born. History educates ("leads outward" in the Latin) in the deepest sense. Of the subjects in the secular curriculum, it is the best at teaching those virtues once reserved for theology—humility in the

face of our limited ability to know, and awe in the face
of the expanse of history.[22]

Are we any closer to understanding what Donald Trump
means by "make America great again"? I think we can be confident about what this phrase means to many of the white
conservative evangelicals who voted for him: America was
great when it was a Christian nation, even if the very idea of
America as a Christian nation rests on shaky historical and
theological ground. Evangelicals should also be careful about
borrowing a phrase that, as Rev. Ray McMillan taught me
several years ago, is at least racially insensitive and at worst
racially offensive. For too many who have been the objects of
white evangelical fear, real American greatness is still something to be hoped for—not something to be recovered from
an imagined past.

CONCLUSION

The evangelical road to Donald Trump has been marked by the politics of fear, power, and nostalgia. While writing this book, I gave some of my preliminary thoughts about evangelicals and Trump in a lecture at a Christian college. Afterwards, a student asked me: "How should Christians respond to the election of Donald Trump? What do you think we are supposed to do?"

It was a fair question. It was also a question that my training as a historian and my research for previous books had not prepared me to answer. History is a limited discipline. Historians provide context for contemporary debates; they explain why things happened the way they did; but they don't usually offer advice or give people plans of action for how to use the information they provide. Realizing that this book has taken me beyond history and into social criticism, I am reminded of the standard attack on critical writing—that is, critics are good at diagnosing problems and bad at offering practical solutions.

Part of my hesitation in responding to this thoughtful student stemmed from my understanding that Christians, many of whom have thought deeply about what a faithful witness in politics might look like, will not always agree on how to vote. Each election is different, with a new set of pressing concerns and a new slate of candidates. Many evangelical voters will always see abortion as the most important issue on the political agenda. But as I suggested in chapter 4, serious evangelicals could respond to this moral problem in diverse ways that may not always lead to an obvious choice of one candidate over another. Other voters will prioritize the campaign against poverty, protecting the environment, protecting traditional family structures, fighting for religious liberty, or energizing the economy as the best way to create economic opportunity for the poor. Different elections in different years may bring different issues to the fore, and thus tip the balance of the evangelical vote. Furthermore, some may vote with a different set of priorities in a presidential election than they would in a local or state race. The diversity of opinion among politically savvy Christians was evident in the personal notes and emails I received after that lecture. Most of my correspondents said virtually nothing about my attempt to place Trump's evangelicals in historical context. Yet all of them spent multiple paragraphs explaining to me how I *should have* answered the student's question about how to respond to the presidency of Trump.

Evangelicals may have carried Donald Trump to the presidency in 2016, but we should probably see his success among these voters as part of a last-ditch attempt—a kind of Pickett's Charge, if you will—to win the culture wars. The average Trump voter is fifty-seven years old; most of his court evangelicals are old and white. Younger evangelicals, the kind that I teach every day, do not seem to share their parents' and grandparents' political playbook. The culture wars are not going well for this latter demographic group. It may be time for those Christians who want to influence public policy to think about what it means to face the future from a position on the periphery rather than from "a seat at the table." A lot of this kind of thinking has already begun.[1]

If you picked up this book and have made it this far, you will not be surprised that I think about evangelical political engagement from the perspective of a historian. While we always need to be careful about taking lessons from the "foreign country" of the past and applying them to contemporary issues, we certainly should not ignore our natural inclination to find a usable past. What kind of historical examples can we find of Christians living faithfully—and engaging politically—from positions located outside the corridors of power and privilege?

In June 2017, I spent ten days with my family and several colleagues from Messiah College traveling through the American South on a civil rights movement bus tour. Our trip took us to some of the most important sites and cities of the movement. We made stops in Greensboro, Atlanta, Albany, Montgomery, Selma, Birmingham, Memphis, and Nashville. Along the way we spent time with some of the veterans of the movement. In Atlanta we heard from Juanita Jones Abernathy, the wife and co-laborer of Ralph Abernathy, one of Martin Luther King Jr.'s closest associates. In Albany we sang civil rights songs with Rutha Mae Harris, one of the original Freedom Singers. In Selma we met Joanne Bland, a local activist who, at the age of eleven, participated in all three Edmund Pettus Bridge marches. In Birmingham we talked with Carolyn Maull McKinstry and Denise McNair. McKinstry was fifteen years old when she survived the Ku Klux Klan bombing of the Sixteenth Street Baptist Church on September 15, 1963. That explosion took the life of McNair's sister, whom she never had a chance to meet. In Nashville, we listened to the inspirational stories of Ernest "Rip" Patton, one of the early freedom riders, and Kwame Leonard, one of the movement's behind-the-scenes organizers.[2]

As I processed everything that I learned on the "Returning to the Roots of Civil Rights" bus tour, I kept returning to thoughts about the relationship between religion and politics. Donald Trump had been in office for under five months, but my anger and frustration upon learning that 81 percent of my fellow evangelicals had voted for him were still fresh. As I listened to the voices of the movement veterans, walked the ground that they had walked, and saw the photographs, studied the exhibits, and watched the footage, it was clear that I was witnessing a Christian approach to politics that was very different from the one that catapulted Trump into the White House. Hope, humility, and a responsible use of American history defined the political engagement and social activism of the civil rights movement.

Therefore, rather than ending this book with an exact prescription for how the 19 percent of white evangelical voters who did not vote for Donald Trump should act while he is in office, I want to conclude by returning to three questions I raised in the introduction to this book. How might evangelical politics change if we replaced fear with hope? How might evangelical politics change if we replaced the pursuit of power with the cultivation of humility? How might evangelical politics change if we replaced nostalgia with history?

Hope, Not Fear

Those who participated in the civil rights movement had much to fear: bombs, burning crosses, billy clubs, death threats, water hoses, police dogs, and lynch mobs—to name a few. They feared for the lives of their families and spent every day wondering whether they would still be around to continue the fight the next day. For these reasons, many African Americans, understandably, did not participate in the movement and prevented their children from getting involved. The danger was very real.

Martin Luther King Jr. knew this. When we visited the old Ebenezer Baptist Church in Atlanta, the church where King was baptized and where he (and his father) served as pastor, his final sermon, the one he delivered in Memphis on April 3, 1968, was playing over the speakers. King was in Memphis to encourage sanitation workers fighting for better pay and improved working conditions. I sat in the back pew and listened:

> Well, I don't know what will happen now. We've got some difficult days ahead. But it really doesn't matter with me now. Because I've been to the mountaintop. And I don't mind. Like anybody, I would like to live a long life. Longevity has its place. But I'm not concerned about that now. I just want to do God's will. And He has allowed me to go up to the mountain. And I've looked over, and I've seen the Promised Land. I may not get there with you, but I want you to know tonight, that we as a people will get to the Promised Land. So I'm happy tonight. I'm not worried about anything. I'm not fearing anything. Mine eyes have seen the glory of the coming of the Lord.

It was a message of hope. Because of his faith, God had given him—and the men and women of the movement he led—all the strength they would need to continue the struggle. King made himself available to do the Lord's will. Now he was looking forward. Was he talking about his eternal life in what now seems like prophetic fashion, or was he talking about God working out his purposes on earth? No matter: King was confident in God's power to work out his will: "Mine eyes have seen the glory of the coming of the Lord." An assassin's bullet took King's life the next day, April 4, 1968, but the movement went on.

Can evangelicals recover this confidence in God's power—not just in his wrath against their enemies but in his ability to work out his purposes for good? Can they recover this hope? The historian Christopher Lasch once wrote this: "Hope does not demand a belief in progress. It demands a belief in justice: a conviction that the wicked will suffer, that wrongs will be made right, that the underlying order of things is not flouted with impunity. Hope implies a deep-seated trust in life that appears absurd to most who lack it."[3] I saw this kind of hope in every place we visited on our trip. It was not mere optimism that things would get better if only we could elect the right candidates. Rather, it was a view of this world, together with an understanding of the world to come, forged amid suffering and pain. Not everyone would make it to the mountaintop on this side of eternity, but God's purposes would be worked out, and eventually they would be able to understand those purposes—if not in this life, surely in the world to come. The people in the movement understood that laws, social programs, even local and voluntary action, would only get them so far. Something deeper was needed. There was something kingdom-oriented going on in these Southern cities. I thought of the words of the Lord's Prayer: "Thy Kingdom come, thy will be done, on earth as it in heaven." I saw this kind of hope in the eyes of Rip Patton as he sat with us in the Nashville Public Library and explained why (and how) he had such a "good time" singing while incarcerated with other freedom riders in Parchman Prison in Jackson, Mississippi. I heard this kind of hope in the voice of Rutha Mae Harris as she led us in "This Little Light of Mine" and "Ain't Gonna Turn Me 'Round" from the front of the sanctuary of the Old Mount Zion Baptist Church in Albany. As I walked across the Edmund Pettus Bridge in Selma, Alabama, I wondered if I could ever muster the courage of John Lewis and Joanne Bland as they marched into the face of terror on Bloody Sunday. Such audacity requires hope.

But too often fear leads to hopelessness, a state of mind that Glenn Tinder has described as a "kind of death." Hopelessness causes us to direct our gaze backward toward worlds we can never recover. It causes us to imagine a future filled with horror. Tyrants focus our attention on the desperate nature of our circumstances and the "carnage" of the social and cultural landscape that they claim to have the power to heal. A kernel of truth, however, always informs such a dark view of life. Poverty is a problem. Rusted-out factories often do appear like "tombstones across the landscape of our nation." Crime is real. But demagogues want us to dwell on the carnage and, to quote Bruce Springsteen, "waste our summer praying in vain for a savior to rise from these streets." Hope, on the other hand, "draws us into the future," and in this way it "engages us in life."[4]

Humility, Not Power

It is nonsensical to talk about the civil rights movement in terms of political power, because even at the height of the movement's influence, African Americans did not possess much political power. Yes, the movement had its leaders, and

they did have time in the national spotlight. But when movement leaders entered the "court," they were usually there to
speak truth to the king, not to flatter him. Martin Luther King
Jr., for example, was willing to break with Lyndon Johnson
when he disagreed with him on the Vietnam War, even if it
meant losing access to the most powerful man on earth.

Most of all, though, the civil rights movement was shaped
by people of humble means who lived ordinary lives in ordinary neighborhoods. Many of them never expected to step
onto a national stage or receive credit for leading the greatest
social movement in American history. These ordinary men
and women fought injustice wherever God had placed them.
And they offer us a beautiful illustration of what James Davison Hunter has called "faithful presence":

> [A] theology of faithful presence first calls Christians
> to attend to the people and places that they experience
> directly. It is not that believers should be disconnected
> from, or avoid responsibility for, people and places
> across the globe. Far from it. . . . But with that said, the
> call of faithful presence gives priority to what is right
> in front of us—community, the neighborhood, and the
> city, and the people in which these are constituted. For
> most, this will mean a preference for stability, local-
> ity, and particularity of place and its needs. It is here,
> through the joys, sufferings, hopes, disappointments,
> concerns, desires, and worries of people with whom
> we are in long-term and close relation—family, neigh-
> bors, co-workers, and community—where we find
> authenticity as a body of believers. It is here where
> we learn forgiveness and humility, practice kindness,
> hospitality, and charity, grow in patience and wisdom,

and become clothed in compassion, gentleness, and joy. This is the crucible within which Christian holiness is forged. This is the context in which shalom is enacted. . . . Faithful presence . . . would encourage ambition, but the instrumentalities of ambition are always subservient to the requirement of humility and charity.[5]

I thought about Hunter's words as I stood in the hot Selma sun and listened to Joanne Bland explain to us the significance of a small and crumbling patch of pavement in a playground behind Brown Chapel AME church. This was the exact spot, she told us, where the 1965 Selma-to-Montgomery marches began. For Bland, who was raised in a housing complex across the street from the church, this was a sacred space.

The humility on display during the civil rights movement was just as countercultural then as it is now. This is usually the case with nonviolent protests. Those who participated thought of themselves not as individuals but as part of a movement larger than themselves. Rip Patton was a twenty-one-year-old music major at Tennessee State University when he met Jim Lawson in 1959. Lawson trained Patton (and others) in nonviolent protest. Soon Patton found himself seated at a lunch counter in downtown Nashville, where he would be spit on, punched, and covered in ketchup, mustard, salt, and water. Patton did not retaliate because he had been educated in the spiritual discipline necessary for a situation like this. Martin Luther King Jr. was leading a political and social movement, but he was also the high priest of a spiritual movement, something akin to a religious revival.

The civil rights movement never spoke the language of hate or resentment. In fact, its Christian leaders saw that all human beings were made in the image of God and sinners in need of God's redemptive love. Many in the movement practiced what theologian Reinhold Niebuhr described as "the spiritual discipline against resentment." They saw that those who retaliated violently or with anger against injustice were only propagating injustices of their own. Instead, the spiritual discipline against resentment unleashed a different kind of power—the power of the cross and the resurrection. This kind of power could provide comfort amid suffering and a faithful gospel witness to the world. The Mississippi voting rights activist Fannie Lou Hamer said it best: "The white man's afraid he'll be treated like he's been treating the Negroes, but I couldn't carry that much hate. It wouldn't have solved any problems for me to hate whites because they hate me. Oh, there's so much hate! Only God has kept the Negro sane."[6]

History, Not Nostalgia

As we saw in chapter 5, many African Americans find American nostalgia troubling because they recognize that there is little in our nation's history to yearn for. The leaders of the civil rights movement could not make appeals to a golden age. They could only look forward with hope. Those in the movement thus had a clear understanding about the differences between history and nostalgia. When they did turn to the past, it was often an appeal to ideals such as liberty, freedom, or justice, ideals written down in our nation's sacred documents that had yet to be applied to them completely. History was a means by which they challenged white Americans to collectively come face to face with the moral contradiction at the heart of their republic. As King said in his April

1968 sermon in Memphis, "All we say to America is, 'Be true to what you said on paper.'" In the process, the movement also challenged white Christians to come to terms with the hypocritical way they practiced their faith. As I listened to the veterans of the civil rights movement tell their stories, I was surprised how often I heard them describe America as a "Christian nation." But this was not the Christian nationalist nostalgia of David Barton, Robert Jeffress, or the court evangelicals. It was a gesture to what they hoped the United States might become.

There is no better example of how movement leaders practiced history than Martin Luther King's "Letter from a Birmingham Jail." King came to Birmingham in April 1963 and led demonstrations calling for an end to segregation and racist hiring practices. He was arrested and spent several days in jail. During his stay in jail he learned from a newspaper smuggled into his cell that eight white Alabama ministers had published a "Call for Unity," a statement that claimed King was an outside agitator intent on disrupting the peace of the city of Birmingham. Steeped in the history of Christianity and the political history of the United States, King started writing his response on scraps of paper, and later finished on a pad provided by his attorney. He said he was in Birmingham because "injustice is here." Justice, King argued, was a universal concept that defined America and thus needed to be defended everywhere. He reminded the Alabama clergymen that Thomas Jefferson and Abraham Lincoln opposed injustice and championed equality. In the United States, he added, civil rights were "God-given." But King also believed that injustice should not be tolerated in a Christian nation. Segregation violated the teachings of Augustine and Aquinas. Shadrach, Meshach, and Abednego championed God's law over the law of King Nebuchadnezzar in the biblical book of Daniel. King announced that he would continue to fight for "what is best in the American Dream and for the most sacred values in our Judeo-Christian heritage, thereby bringing our nation back to those great wells of democracy which were dug deep by the founding fathers in their formulation of the Constitution and the Declaration of Independence."[7]

White evangelicals can learn much from the way King uses history in his "Letter from a Birmingham Jail." The early civil rights movement needed its leaders to have a working knowledge of American history, but these leaders did not use the past as fodder for a national reclamation project. They knew there was little to reclaim. Instead, they used the past as a means of moving forward in hope and calling the church and the nation to live up to the principles they were built on. While many white Americans today succumb to the narcissism that tells them that their place in the story of the nation is not worth serious reflection, King and his followers had a clear-eyed understanding of the past. They desperately wanted to be grafted into this imperfect but hopeful story, and to contribute their gifts and talents to the writing of future chapters of that story.

Where does all of this reflection leave us? How might hope, humility, and history inform the way we white American evangelicals think about politics and other forms of public engagement? I hope that what I have written here might spur conversations and initiatives born out of possible answers to this question. Evangelicals can do better than Donald Trump. His campaign and presidency have drawn on a troubling pattern of American evangelicalism that is willing to yield to old habits grounded in fear, nostalgia, and the search for power.

Too many of its leaders (and their followers) have traded their Christian witness for a mess of political pottage and a few federal judges. It should not surprise us that people are leaving evangelicalism or no longer associating themselves with that label—or, in some cases, leaving the church altogether.

It's time to take a long hard look at what we have become. Believe me, we have a lot of work to do.

Believe me.

POSTSCRIPT TO THE
PAPERBACK EDITION

Since Eerdmans released *Believe Me: The Evangelical Road to Donald Trump* in June 2018, I have talked about evangelicals and Donald Trump to thousands of people who came to public events devoted to the book, responded to my television and radio appearances, and reached out via social media. I have had conversations—some of them quite long and intense—with Donald Trump voters, Hillary Clinton voters, and those who did not vote for either candidate in 2016. The book has resonated with secular audiences, mainline Protestant groups, and evangelical Christians.

Eighteen months later, I would not change anything about the core argument of *Believe Me*. Unlike many other books about Trump and evangelicals, this book takes a long view. As a historian I study change over time, but I also call attention to the continuity between past and present. The embrace of Donald Trump is the latest manifestation of an evangelical approach to politics and public life that is three centuries old.

Trump has now been president for three years. His support among conservative evangelicals has not wavered. Fear, the pursuit of power, and nostalgia for a world that is gone and is never coming back continue to motivate evangelicals who support our forty-fifth president. I fully expect evangelicals to rally around Trump again in 2020. For the reasons I suggested in this book, they are the most reliable part of his political base.

I have also learned a lot about evangelicalism and politics during my conversations with *Believe Me* readers. Here are four of those lessons:

First, white evangelicals who voted for Trump in 2016 and continue to support him are not a monolithic group. For example, many Trump evangelicals like the president because he is willing to reject political correctness, fight the "liberals" trying to undermine Christian America, bring manufacturing jobs back to the United States, and keep America white through immigration restrictions and the construction of a wall on the Mexican border. Many who fall into this category hate Hillary Clinton (at least two evangelical attendees at a book talk wanted to "lock her up"). They came to my talks and lectures with red "Make America Great Again" caps and did not hesitate to tell me about the sense of community they have experienced while attending Trump rallies. They offered me a political cocktail that mixes Bible verses (usually taken out of context) with the punditry of Sean Hannity and Rush Limbaugh. Like Robert Jeffress and Jerry Falwell Jr., these evangelicals supported Donald Trump during the 2016 GOP primaries, choosing the New York businessperson over Christian Right candidates such as Ted Cruz or Ben Carson.

Some evangelicals believe that support for Trump is a way of exercising obedience to God. Trump is the chosen one, a new King Cyrus, a vessel sent by God to restore America to its Christian roots and defend the political interests of the born again. These evangelicals are so certain about such a providential interpretation of our current president's role in human history because it came from anointed prophets, many of them affiliated with the rapidly growing Independent Network Charismatic Movement.

Another significant group of evangelicals chose Donald Trump in 2016 because he was the lesser of two evils. Their disdain for Hillary Clinton is strong, but so is their revulsion to Trump's tweets, racist remarks, nativist policies, misogynistic comments, narcissism, and endless lies. In the end, these evangelicals—many of them thoughtful and well-educated men and women—voted for Trump because they believed he would execute the Christian Right playbook that I wrote about in chapter 2. Most of these voters would reject the label "Trump supporter," but they also felt vindicated about pulling the lever for the GOP nominee in 2016 after he appointed Neil Gorsuch and Brett Kavanaugh to the Supreme Court. These voters rarely talk about the fact that their vote in 2016 makes them partially responsible for Trump's immoral presidency, the damage it is doing to our republican institutions, and the potential harm it will have for the witness of the gospel in the nation and the world.

Second, I learned firsthand that there are many people, very few of whom voted for Donald Trump, who are deeply troubled about the state of evangelical Christianity in America. I heard stories of men and women scarred by experiences with authoritarian, politically driven evangelical Christianity. Some have left evangelicalism for Protestant mainline denominations. Others have left Christianity entirely. Still others are in search of a more hopeful Christianity. Evangelical pastors are wondering how they can minister to congregations divided by politics. A few of them told me that their pastoral counseling load has increased since Trump's election as some members of their congregations try to make sense of how so many of their fellow believers could support this president. Needless to say, very few of these people voted for Donald Trump.

Night after night, men and women waited in line for me to sign their books and to tell me their stories. One young father, wiping tears from his face, expressed to me how much he appreciated meeting like-minded people in the audience at a *Believe Me* book event. He described the conversation he had as freeing and confessed that he did not feel comfortable starting such discussions in his local evangelical church. A woman told me that she felt ostracized by her congregation and pastor after telling people she did not vote for Trump. Many said that it was refreshing to hear an evangelical speak about hope and humility in a lecture on political engagement. Some of these conversations continued late into the evening. I did my best to offer encouragement, join in their lament, and, on a few occasions, pray with them. Most of the time I just listened.

Third, I learned that Donald Trump disgusts plenty of evangelical young people. The Christian college students I met remain committed to conservative social values, and many still affiliate with the Republican Party, but they are largely appalled by Trump's immigration and environmental policies and sickened by what they see as the hypocrisy of an older generation who support such a president. Most of my formal and informal conversations with evangelical millennials and Gen Zers revealed either a general malaise about politics or an authentic interest in rethinking evangelical political engagement in a way that moves us beyond the culture-war playbook.

Fourth, and finally, I was unprepared for the level of anti-intellectualism I would encounter among many (though certainly not all) Trump evangelicals. I knew from reading Mark Noll's book *The Scandal of the Evangelical Mind* that anti-intellectualism has become a defining characteristic of American evangelicalism, but my engagement with Trump-supporting evangelicals made me realize that few of the president's supporters are open to engaging with rational arguments rooted in American history and political philosophy. Do not get me wrong: I have been encouraged by the notes from evangelicals who have indeed wrestled with the arguments in the book and even in some cases changed their minds about Trump after reading it. The stories of men and women who have taken the ideas in this book and used them in discussions with evangelical friends and family members who voted for Trump have buoyed my spirits. However, in a world of social media echo chambers and Fox News, I now realize that I placed too much trust in the power of rational argument and historical thinking.

I never wanted *Believe Me* to speak solely to those outside the evangelical fold. I had no interest in preaching to the anti-Trump choir. Nor did I assume that everyone would agree with the argument of *Believe Me*. But I did hope my words might reach Trump voters and perhaps convince a few of them that they made a mistake in 2016. I thought Trump-supporting evangelicals might be willing, through dialogue, to open their minds to an alternative way of thinking about political engagement. Too often, I was wrong.

There is still much work to do.

John Fea
August 24, 2019

NOTES

NOTES TO THE INTRODUCTION

1. James Davison Hunter, *To Change the World: The Irony, Tragedy, and Possibility of Christianity in the Late Modern World* (New York: Oxford University Press, 2010), 234, 280.

2. Sarah Pulliam Bailey, "Donald Trump Almost Puts Money in the Communion Plate at a Church in Iowa," *Washington Post*, February 1, 2016, https://www.washingtonpost.com/news/acts-of-faith/wp/2016/02/01/donald-trump-accidentally-put-money-in-the-communion-plate-at-a-church-in-iowa/?utm_term=.733f0419ea8e.

3. "Trump Female Base Holds Despite Allegations," accessed January 30, 2018, via YouTube at https://www.youtube.com/watch?v=Z6PbPFBPs3k.

4. According to political scientist Tobin Grant, when pollsters talk about "evangelicals," what they "really mean are 'white, non-Hispanic Protestants.'" Polls, of course, are not perfect, and this is particularly true when it comes to religion. The 81 percent is based on a voter's self-description as "born-again or evangelical Christian." It says nothing about the theological or spiritual content of that voter's faith, or whether he or she attends church on a regular basis. As a result, the number of devout, theologically orthodox, born-again, weekly-church-

going evangelicals who voted for Donald Trump is probably lower than
81 percent. With all of this in mind, I want to offer three caveats related
to how I use the term "evangelical" in this book. First, I am referring
exclusively to *white* evangelicals. Black and Hispanic evangelicals did not
vote for Donald Trump in such large numbers. Second, if the number of
white evangelical voters who voted for Trump is indeed lower than 81
percent, the real number (which is virtually impossible to nail down) is
still quite large and thus does little to undermine the essential premise
of this book. Third, whether the evangelicals who voted for Trump are
regular church-going, born-again Christians or nonpracticing cultural
Christians who simply claimed the label "evangelical" during the exit
poll, they still made a public declaration of their religious identity, which
I take seriously. The message of this book thus applies to both groups,
though I imagine people who practice their evangelical faith might
take it more seriously. See Tobin Grant, "How the Polls Inflate Trump's
Evangelical Vote," *Colorado Springs Gazette* (distributed through Religion
News Service), August 3, 2016, http://gazette.com/how-the-polls-inflate
-trumps-evangelical-vote/article/1581884; see also Sarah Pulliam Bailey,
"White Evangelicals Voted Overwhelmingly for Donald Trump," *Washington Post*, November 9, 2016, https://www.washingtonpost.com/news/
acts-of-faith/wp/2016/11/09/exit-polls-show-white-evangelicals-voted
-overwhelmingly-for-donald-trump/?utm_term=.78bf4840c163.

5. Robert P. Jones, *The End of White Christian America* (New York: Simon and Schuster; reprint ed., 2017).

6. Christopher Lasch, *The True and Only Heaven: Progress and Its Critics* (New York: Norton, 1991), 118.

7. Marilynne Robinson, "Fear," *New York Review of Books*, September 24, 2015, http://www.nybooks.com/articles/2015/09/24/
marilynne-robinson-fear/.

8. Glenn Tinder, *The Fabric of Hope: An Essay* (Grand Rapids: Eerdmans, 1999), 168.

9. These references come from a YouTube video montage of Trump
campaign speeches, posted by TheTColl, "Ultimate Donald Trump Believe
Me Compilation," YouTube, June 30, 2016, https://www.youtube.com/
watch?v=zDTeMNhuPTc.

10. "Remarks by President Trump at National Prayer Breakfast,"

Whitehouse.gov, February 2, 2017, https://www.whitehouse.gov/the
-press-office/2017/02/02/remarks-president-trump-national-prayer
-breakfast.

11. Donald Trump speech at 2016 Values Voter Summit, posted by
FRCAction, YouTube, September 9, 2016, https://www.youtube.com/
watch?v=T6ZleOb7gz0.

NOTES TO CHAPTER 1

1. On Carson's lead among evangelicals in September and October
2015, see Philip Bump, "The Irony of Trump's Embrace of White Evangelical Voters," *Washington Post*, October 17, 2017, https://www.washington
post.com/news/politics/wp/2017/10/17/the-irony-of-trumps-embrace
-of-white-evangelical-voters/?utm_term=.da3584ea3831.

2. "Burleigh" (pseudonym), *Connecticut Courant*, July 7, 1800.

3. On fear and political ads see Ted Brader, *Campaigning for Hearts
and Minds: Emotional Appeals in Political Ads Work* (Chicago: University
of Chicago Press, 2006).

4. Jason C. Bivins, *Religion of Fear: The Politics of Horror in Conservative
Evangelicalism* (New York: Oxford University Press, 2008), 26; Martha
Nussbaum, *The New Religious Intolerance: Overcoming Politics of Fear in
an Anxious Age* (Cambridge, MA: Harvard University Press, 2012); Corey
Robin, *Fear: The History of a Political Idea* (New York: Oxford University
Press, 2004), 27, 33, 43; Scott Bader-Saye, *Following Jesus in a Culture of Fear*
(Grand Rapids: Brazos, 2007), 15; Zack Beauchamp, "You're More Likely
to Be Killed by Your Own Clothes Than by an Immigrant Terrorist,"
VOX, June 26, 2017, https://www.vox.com/2016/9/13/12901950/terrorism
-immigrants-clothes; Dan Bobkoff, Dave Mosher, and Skye Gould,
"Trump's Speech Highlighted Victims of Crimes by Immigrants—but a
Look at the Data Shows It's Incredibly Rare," *Business Insider*, March 1,
2017, http://www.businessinsider.com/trump-voice-office-for-victims
-of-immigrant-crime-numbers-not-necessary-2017-3.

5. Nussbaum, *The New Religious Intolerance*, 20–21; Marc Fisher,
John Woodrow Cox, and Peter Hermann, "Pizzagate: From Rumor, to
Hashtag, to Gunfire in D.C.," *Washington Post*, December 6, 2016, https://
www.washingtonpost.com/local/pizzagate-from-rumor-to-hashtag-to

-gunfire-in-dc/2016/12/06/4c7def50-bbd4-11e6-94ac-3d324840106c_
story.html?utm_term=.f9579b1e417d.

6. Andrew Kaczynski and Paul LeBlanc, "GOP Senate Candidate Roy
Moore Has Said He Doesn't Believe Obama Is a Natural Born Citizen,"
CNN, August 23, 2017, http://www.cnn.com/2017/08/22/politics/kfile
-roy-moore-birther-comments/index.html.

7. Gregory A. Smith and David Masci, "Exit Polls and the Evangelical Vote: A Closer Look," Pew Research Center, March 14, 2016,
http://www.pewresearch.org/fact-tank/2016/03/14/exit-polls-and
-the-evangelical-vote-a-closer-look/; Josh Clinton and Carrie Roush,
"Poll: Persistent Partisan Divide over 'Birther' Question," NBC News,
August 10, 2016, https://www.nbcnews.com/politics/2016-election/poll
-persistent-partisan-divide-over-birther-question-n627446.

8. Dinesh D'Souza, "How Obama Thinks," *Forbes*, September 9,
2010, https://www.forbes.com/forbes/2010/0927/politics-socialism
-capitalism-private-enterprises-obama-business-problem.html. At
the time he wrote this article, D'Souza was the president of The Kings
College in New York City. He would later develop his views in the
best-selling *The Roots of Obama's Rage* (Washington, DC: Regnery, 2011).
On Gingrich, see Philip Bump, "A History of President Obama Being
Called 'Anti-colonial,'" *Washington Post*, February 20, 2015, https://
www.washingtonpost.com/news/the-fix/wp/2015/02/20/a-history-of
-president-obama-being-called-anti-colonial/?utm_term=.75caf3ffe8ab.
On historical thinking and the uses of evidence, see John Fea, *Why Study
History? Reflecting on the Importance of the Past* (Grand Rapids: Baker Ac-
ademic, 2013).

9. Jennifer Agiesta, "Misperceptions Persist about Obama's
Faith, but Aren't So Widespread," CNN, September 14, 2015, http://
www.cnn.com/2015/09/13/politics/barack-obama-religion-christian
-misperceptions/index.html. See also John Fea, "The 'Obama Is a Muslim' Trump Card," *Al Jazeera America*, September 22, 2015, http://america
.aljazeera.com/opinions/2015/9/the-obama-is-a-muslim-trump-card
.html.

10. Cheryl K. Chumley, "Franklin Graham: Obama 'Only Knows Islam, and He Has Given a Pass to Islam,'" *Washington Times*, February
18, 2015, http://www.washingtontimes.com/news/2015/feb/18/franklin

-graham-obama-only-knows-islam-and-he-has-/; Dom Giordano, "Dr. Richard Land: Pres. Obama Has His Head in the Ground When It Comes to Radical Islamic Jihadism and ISIS," CBS Philly, February 17, 2015, http://philadelphia.cbslocal.com/2015/02/17/dr-richard-land-pres -obama-has-his-head-in-the-ground-when-it-comes-to-radical-islamic -jihadism-and-isis/. On the history of evangelical anti-Islamic rhetoric, see Thomas Kidd, *American Christians and Islam: Evangelical Culture and Muslims from the Colonial Period to the Age of Terrorism* (Princeton, NJ: Princeton University Press, 2008).

11. John Fea, "Would You Vote for This Man?" Patheos.com, February 15, 2012, http://www.patheos.com/resources/additional-resources/2012/02/ vote-for-this-man-john-fea-02-15-2012.

12. "What We Believe," Website of Trinity United Church of Christ, accessed November 4, 2017, https://trinitychicago.org/statement-of -faith/.

13. Gregory A. Smith and Jessica Martinez, "How the Faithful Voted: A Preliminary 2016 Analysis," Pew Research Center, November 9, 2016, http://www.pewresearch.org/fact-tank/2016/11/09/how-the-faithful -voted-a-preliminary-2016-analysis/.

14. "Barack Obama on Abortion Policy at the Saddleback Civil Forum," Website of the Berkley Center for Religion, Peace and World Affairs, August 16, 2008, https://berkleycenter.georgetown.edu/quotes/ barack-obama-on-abortion-policy-at-the-saddleback-civil-forum.

15. Ronald J. Sider, *The Scandal of Evangelical Politics* (Grand Rapids: Baker, 2008), 19.

16. H. R. 3396 (104th): Defense of Marriage Act, Govtrack Website, accessed November 4, 2017, https://www.govtrack.us/congress/ bills/104/hr3396/text.

17. Charlie Savage and Sheryl Gay Stolberg, "In Shift, U.S. Says Marriage Act Blocks Gay Rights," *New York Times*, February 23, 2011, http:// www.nytimes.com/2011/02/24/us/24marriage.html?pagewanted=all; "Transcript: Robin Roberts ABC News Interview with President Obama," ABC News, May 9, 2012, http://abcnews.go.com/Politics/transcript-robin -roberts-abc-news-interview-president-obama/story?id=16316043.

18. "Supreme Court Redefines Marriage," Website of the National Association of Evangelicals, June 26, 2015, https://www.nae.net/supreme

-court-redefines-marriage/; John Stonestreet, "Christian Leaders Re-spond to Obergefell vs. Hodges: A Symposium," *Breakpoint*, June 26, 2015, http://www.breakpoint.org/2015/06/christian-leaders-respond-to-obergefell-vs-hodges-a-symposium/; Rev. Samuel Rodriguez, "State-ment by Rev. Samuel Rodriguez on SCOTUS Same-Sex Marriage Ruling," *ALR*, June 26, 2015, http://alarryross.com/statement-by-rev-samuel-rodriguez-on-scotus-same-sex-marriage-ruling/.

19. Rod Dreher, *The Benedict Option: A Strategy for Christians in a Post-Christian Nation* (New York: Sentinel, 2017).

20. Robert P. Jones, *The End of White Christian America* (New York: Simon and Schuster, 2017), 144–45.

21. Kate Tracy, "Gordon College Loses City Contract, Gets Accredita-tion Scrutiny," *Christianity Today*, July 14, 2014, http://www.christianity today.com/news/2014/july/gordon-college-loses-city-contract-gets-accreditation-scrut.html.

22. Jones, *End of White Christian America*, 120.

23. Jones, *End of White Christian America*, 85.

24. Betsy Woodruff, "Why Evangelicals Worship Trump," *The Daily Beast*, August 21, 2015, https://www.thedailybeast.com/why-evangelicals-worship-trump.

25. Maeve Reston and Theodore Schleifer, "Carson Questions Au-thenticity of Trump's Faith," CNN, September 9, 2015, http://www.cnn .com/2015/09/09/politics/ben-carson-donald-trump-faith/index.html.

26. Jenna Johnson and Abigail Hauslohner, "'I Think Islam Hates Us': A Timeline of Trump's Comments on Islam and Muslims," *Wash-ington Post*, May 20, 2017, https://www.washingtonpost.com/news/post -politics/wp/2017/05/20/i-think-islam-hates-us-a-timeline-of-trumps -comments-about-islam-and-muslims/?utm_term=.7a865962f370.

27. "Ben Carson Resists Challenges to the Life Story He Rode to Po-litical Prominence," *New York Times*, November 6, 2015, https://www .nytimes.com/politics/first-draft/2015/11/06/ben-carson-west-point/?_ r=0; Trip Gabriel, "Ben Carson Is Struggling to Grasp Foreign Policy, Ad-visers Say," *New York Times*, November 17, 2015, https://www.nytimes .com/2015/11/18/us/politics/ben-carson-is-struggling-to-grasp-foreign -policy-advisers-say.html.

28. Jamie Dean, "Ballot Boxing: Rubio Gets New Religious Advis-

ers," *WORLD*, January 5, 2016, https://world.wng.org/2016/01/ballot_
boxing_rubio_gets_new_religious_advisers; John Fea, "Rubio's Appeal
to Iowa Evangelicals," *The Way of Improvement Leads Home*, January 7,
2016, https://thewayofimprovement.com/2016/01/07/rubios-appeal-to
-iowa-evangelicals/. The board also included a rabbi and several Roman
Catholics, including Stanford University law professor Michael McCon-
nell, a scholar whom George W. Bush had once seriously considered as
a Supreme Court nominee.

29. John Fea, "Evangelicals Are the Prize in S.C.," *USA Today*, February 16, 2016, https://www.usatoday.com/story/opinion/2016/02/16/
evangelicals-south-carolina-republican-primary-column/80414280/;
Brad Christerson and Richard Flory, *The Rise of Network Christianity:
How Independent Leaders Are Changing the Religious Landscape* (New
York: Oxford University Press, 2017), 100, 136; Ben Schreckinger, "Donald Trump's Saving Grace: Televangelists," *Politico*, September 30, 2015,
https://www.politico.com/story/2015/09/donald-trumps-evangelicals
-televangelists-214250.

30. David Brooks, "The Brutalism of Ted Cruz," *New York Times*,
January 12, 2016, https://www.nytimes.com/2016/01/12/opinion/
the-brutalism-of-ted-cruz.html?_r=0; Laura Premack, "Trump and
Cruz Battle for Evangelical Hearts," *Boston Review*, January 29, 2016,
http://bostonreview.net/us/laura-premack-donald-trump-ted-cruz
-evangelical-christians; John Fea, "Ted Cruz's Campaign Is Fueled by a
Dominionist Vision for America," *Washington Post* (distributed by Religion News Service), February 4, 2016, https://www.washingtonpost
.com/national/religion/ted-cruzs-campaign-is-fueled-by-a-dominionist
-vision-for-america-commentary/2016/02/04/86373158-cb6a-11e5
-b9ab-26591104bb19_story.html?utm_term=.6d09c49e9d42; Kyle Mantyla, "Glenn Beck: If Ted Cruz Loses Indiana, We 'Lose Freedom for All
Mankind,'" Right Wing Watch, April 27, 2016, http://www.rightwing
watch.org/post/glenn-beck-if-ted-cruz-loses-indiana-we-lose-freedom
-for-all-mankind/.

31. "Ted Cruz Speaks at a Rally at Faith Assembly of God Church,
Orlando, FL," November 13, 2015, http://www.youtube.com/watch?v=
rBaVJTddzlo.

32. Fea, "Ted Cruz's Campaign . . ."; "Ted Cruz Speaks to Evangeli-

cals at a Christian Book Store," "The Circus" (SHOWTIME television), accessed via You Tube on January 31, 2018, https://www.youtube.com/watch?v=XFhvNmHL6iU.

33. Tal Kopan, "Ted Cruz Releases Supreme Court Ad after Justice Antonin Scalia's Death," CNN Politics, February 15, 2016, http://www.cnn.com/2016/02/15/politics/ted-cruz-justice-antonin-scalia-supreme-court-ad/index.html; Matt Flegenheimer, "Ted Cruz: 'We Are One Justice Away from the Second Amendment Being Written Out of the Constitution,'" *New York Times,* February 14, 2016, https://www.nytimes.com/live/supreme-court-justice-antonin-scalia-dies-at-79/cruz-we-are-one-justice-away-from-the-second-amendment-being-written-out-of-the-constitution/; Alexis Levinson, "Cruz Promises Relief from a Grave Future," *National Review,* February 18, 2016, http://www.nationalreview.com/corner/431574/cruz-promises-relief-grave-future.

34. Julie Lyons, "Robert Jeffress Wants a 'Mean Son of a Gun' for President," *Dallas Observer,* April 5, 2016, http://www.dallasobserver.com/news/robert-jeffress-wants-a-mean-son-of-a-gun-for-president-says-trump-isnt-a-racist-8184721.

35. Kate Shellnutt, "Most White Evangelicals Don't Believe Muslims Belong in America," *Christianity Today,* July 26, 2017, http://www.christianitytoday.com/news/2017/july/pew-how-white-evangelicals-view-us-muslims-islam.html.

36. Transcript of Donald Trump Speech at Liberty University, CNN, accessed November 18, 2017, http://transcripts.cnn.com/TRANSCRIPTS/1601/18/ath.01.html.

37. Bivins, *Religion of Fear,* 200; Jones, *End of White Christian America,* 247. Trump's protectionist economic policies and promise to bring back American jobs almost certainly played a role in his evangelical support. Perhaps Trump attracted white, working-class evangelicals in the same way that he attracted white, working-class non-evangelicals. It is certainly possible that the reason many of the evangelicals chose Trump over the other GOP candidates was that, when faced with a choice between candidates with similar convictions on moral issues, the voters saw Trump's economic policies as making the difference. I am certainly willing to entertain such a proposal if more data were to be made available.

NOTES TO CHAPTER 2

1. Scott Bader-Saye, *Following Jesus in a Culture of Fear* (Grand Rapids: Brazos, 2007), 79.

2. John Fea, "Heard Yesterday in My Evangelical Church," *The Way of Improvement Leads Home*, October 30, 2017, https://thewayofimprovement .com/2017/10/30/heard-yesterday-in-my-evangelical-church/.

3. Will Herberg, *Protestant, Catholic, Jew: An Essay in American Religious Sociology* (Garden City, NY: Doubleday, 1955).

4. John Fea, *Was America Founded as a Christian Nation? A Historical Introduction* (Louisville: Westminster John Knox, 2011), 51–53.

5. Daniel T. Rodgers, *The Age of Fracture* (Cambridge, MA: Harvard University Press, 2011); James Davison Hunter, *Culture Wars: The Struggle to Control the Family, Art, Education, Law, and Politics in America* (New York: Basic Books, 1991).

6. James Hudnut-Beumler, *Looking for God in the Suburbs: The Religion of the American Dream and Its Critics, 1945–1965* (New Brunswick, NJ: Rutgers University Press, 1994), 31–37; Kevin M. Kruse, *One Nation Under God: How Corporate America Invented Christian America* (New York: Basic Books, 2015), 68, 91.

7. Daniel K. Williams, *God's Own Party: The Making of the Christian Right* (New York: Oxford University Press, 2010), 62.

8. Philip Hamburger, *Separation of Church and State* (Cambridge, MA: Harvard University Press, 2002), 454–57.

9. "*Longinqua*: Encyclical of Pope Leo XIII on Catholicism in the United States, January 6, 1895," Vatican Website, accessed November 25, 2017, http://w2.vatican.va/content/leo-xiii/en/encyclicals/documents/hf _l-xiii_enc_06011895_longinqua.html; Jay P. Dolan, *The American Catholic Experience: A History from Colonial Times to the Present* (New York: Doubleday, 1985), 351–83.

10. Hamburger, *Separation of Church and State*, 461–65, 477. In *McCollum v. Board of Education* (1948), the Supreme Court decided that a school release program to provide religious instruction for Protestant, Catholic, and Jewish students violated the disestablishment clause. In his majority opinion, Black referred to *Everson v. Board*. According to Hamburger, the decision in *McCollum* led many Protestants to "reconsider separation"

as they "now suddenly found themselves confronted with a secular version." Protestants wondered whether "they faced a greater threat from secularism and separation than from Catholicism."

11. John Witte Jr., *Religion and the American Constitutional Experiment* (Boulder, CO: Westview Press, 2005), 205; Kruse, *One Nation Under God*, 170-74.

12. Kruse, *One Nation Under God*, 183-89; Williams, *God's Own Party*, 63.

13. Kruse, *One Nation Under God*, 200, 228-37; Williams, *God's Own Party*, 64-67; John Fea, *The Bible Cause: A History of the American Bible Society* (New York: Oxford University Press, 2015), 233-36.

14. Donna R. Gabaccia, *Immigration and American Diversity: A Social and Cultural History* (Malden, MA: Blackwell Publishers, 2002), 215.

15. Gabaccia, *Immigration and American Diversity*, 236, 252, 254.

16. Mark Noll, *God and Race in American Politics: A Short History* (Princeton, NJ: Princeton University Press, 2008), 156-61.

17. Randall Balmer, *Thy Kingdom Come: An Evangelical's Lament* (New York: Basic Books, 2006), 13-15; Williams, *God's Own Party*, 85.

18. Daniel K. Williams, *Defenders of the Unborn: The Pro-Life Movement before Roe v. Wade* (New York: Oxford University Press, 2016), 197-208.

19. John Fea, *Was America Founded as a Christian Nation? A Historical Introduction* (Louisville: Westminster John Knox, 2011), 57-75.

20. Fea, *Was America Founded as a Christian Nation?*, 55-56; Williams, *God's Own Party*, 138-43; Barry Hankins, *Francis Schaeffer and the Shaping of Evangelical America* (Grand Rapids: Eerdmans, 2008). On Reconstructionism, see Michael McVicar, *Christian Reconstruction: R.J. Rushdoony and American Religious Conservatism* (Chapel Hill: University of North Carolina Press, 2015).

21. Williams, *God's Own Party*, 171-79; Balmer, *Thy Kingdom Come*, 13-15. As I have argued above, if one takes a longer view than Balmer does, it is clear that opposition to desegregation was one of several factors contributing to the birth of the Christian Right.

22. Williams, *God's Own Party*, 171-79, 1; "Republican Party Platform of 1980," *The American Presidency Project*, July 15, 1980, http://www.presidency.ucsb.edu/ws/index.php?pid=25844.

23. Hunter, *To Change the World*, 12.

24. "The Clinton Chronicles," Citizens' Video Press, 1994, can be watched at https://www.youtube.com/watch?v=iWF5SRGEGIs; Lois Romano, "A Core Collection of Clinton Enemies," *Washington Post*, March 2, 1998, https://www.washingtonpost.com/archive/politics/1998/03/02/a-core-collection-of-clinton-enemies/a925d975-782b-4a2b-b4ec-268233551e4d/?utm_term=.f8d3dee86408; Philip Weiss, "Clinton Crazy," *New York Times Magazine*, February 23, 1997, http://www.nytimes.com/1997/02/23/magazine/clinton-crazy.html; Williams, *God's Own Party*, 240–44.

25. Cited in David Van Biema, "Can Falwell Pass His Own Leadership Test?" *Time*, March 23, 1998, p. 34; Gary Bauer, "Clinton Corrupts Our National Culture," *Human Events*, September 25, 1998, 1–2.

26. James Dobson, online letter, December 1998. http://ontology.buffalo.edu/smith/clinton/character.html. I am grateful to Katie and Devin Manzullo-Thomas for bringing this letter to my attention in June 2016.

27. On Pence's strong connection to the evangelical community and the Christian Right, see McKay Coppins, "God's Plan for Mike Pence," *The Atlantic*, January/February 2018, https://www.theatlantic.com/magazine/archive/2018/01/gods-plan-for-mike-pence/546569/.

28. Kate Shellnutt and Sarah Eekhoff-Zylstra, "Who's Who of Trump's 'Tremendous' Faith Advisers," *Christianity Today*, June 22, 2016, http://www.christianitytoday.com/ct/2016/june-web-only/whos-who-of-trumps-tremendous-faith-advisors.html; Jenna Johnson and Robert Barnes, "Donald Trump Releases List of 11 Potential Supreme Court Nominees," *Washington Post*, May 18, 2016, https://www.washingtonpost.com/news/post-politics/wp/2016/05/18/donald-trump-releases-list-of-11-potential-supreme-court-nominees/?utm_term=.85509ea168d0; John Fea, "The No. 1 Reason Evangelicals Still Put Their Hopes in Trump," *Religion News Service*, August 9, 2016, http://religionnews.com/2016/08/09/the-no-1-reason-evangelicals-still-put-their-hopes-in-trump/; "Evangelicals Rally to Trump, Religious 'Nones' Back Clinton," Pew Research Center, July 13, 2016, http://www.pewforum.org/2016/07/13/evangelicals-rally-to-trump-religious-nones-back-clinton/.

29. Lucia Graves and Sam Morris, "The Trump Allegations," *The Guardian*, November 29, 2017, https://www.theguardian.com/us-news/

ng-interactive/2017/nov/30/donald-trump-sexual-misconduct
-allegations-full-list.

30. Sarah Pulliam Bailey, "'Lecherous and Worthless': Megachurch Pastor from Trump's Own Evangelical Council Denounces Him," *Washington Post*, October 10, 2016, https://www.washingtonpost.com/news/ acts-of-faith/wp/2016/10/10/misogynistic-trash-megachurch-pastor -from-trumps-own-evangelical-council-denounces-him/?utm_term =.2a6e3cbdc948.

31. Sarah Pulliam Bailey, "'Still the Best Candidate': Some Evangelicals Still Back Trump Despite Lewd Video," *Washington Post*, October 8, 2016, https://www.washingtonpost.com/news/acts-of-faith/wp/2016/10 /08/still-the-best-candidate-some-evangelicals-still-back-trump -despite-lewd-video/?utm_term=.bc15755654fe.

32. Dennis Thompson, "Constitutional Character: Virtues and Vices in Presidential Leadership," *Presidential Studies Quarterly* 40, no. 1 (March 2010): 23–37. For another treatment of character, see James Davison Hunter, *The Death of Character: Moral Education in an Age without Good or Evil* (New York: Basic Books, 2001).

33. Eric Metaxas, *If You Can Keep It: The Forgotten Promise of American Liberty* (New York: Viking, 2016), 149–80.

34. John Adams, "A Dissertation on the Canon and Feudal Law, 1765," *Digital History*, accessed December 3, 2017, http://www.digitalhistory.uh .edu/disp_textbook.cfm?smtID=3&psid=4118.

35. "The Federalist Papers: No. 57, 1788," The Avalon Project, Yale University Law School, accessed December 3, 2017, http://avalon.law.yale .edu/18th_century/fed57.asp.

36. "The Federalist Papers: No 68, 1788," The Avalon Project, Yale University Law School, accessed December 3, 2017, http://avalon.law .yale.edu/18th_century/fed68.asp.

37. Ruth Graham, "Why Hillary Clinton Bombed with White Evangelical Voters," *Slate*, December 15, 2016, http://www.slate.com/articles/ news_and_politics/politics/2016/12/why_hillary_clinton_bombed_ with_evangelical_voters.html.

38. Quoted in Eliza Collins, "Hillary Clinton: Planned Parenthood Videos 'Disturbing,'" *Politico*, July 29, 2015, https://www.politico.com/

story/2015/07/hillary-clinton-questions-planned-parenthood-videos
-disturbing-120768.

39. John Inazu, *Confident Pluralism: Surviving and Thriving through
Deep Difference* (Chicago: University of Chicago Press, 2016). Inazu argues that "we can and must live together peaceably in spite of deep and
sometimes irresolvable differences over politics, religion, sexuality, and
other important matters. We can do so in two important ways—by in-
sisting on constitutional commitments that honor and protect difference
and by embodying tolerance, humility, and patience in our speech, our
collective action (protests, strikes, and boycotts) and our relationships
across difference." John Inazu, personal website, accessed December 2,
2017, http://johninazu.com/.

NOTES TO CHAPTER 3

1. Neal Gabler, "Why the Trump Era Won't Pass without Serious
Damage to America," *TruthDig*, December 17, 2017, https://www.truthdig
.com/articles/trump-era-wont-pass-without-serious-damage-america/.
Thanks to Phillip Luke Sinitiere for bringing Gabler's quote to my
attention.

2. Richard M. Gamble, *In Search of the City on a Hill: The Making
and Unmaking of an American Myth* (New York: Continuum, 2012), 55–
56, 67; Robert Tracy McKenzie, "A City upon a Hill," Faith and History
(blog), January 7, 2013, https://faithandamericanhistory.wordpress
.com/2013/01/07/a-city-upon-a-hill/.

3. Gamble, *In Search of the City on a Hill*, 60–67.

4. Darrett B. Rutman, *Winthrop's Boston: A Portrait of a Puritan Town,
1630–1649* (Chapel Hill: University of North Carolina Press, 1969).

5. Richard Gildrie, *The Profane, the Civil, and the Godly: The Reformation of Manners in Orthodox New England, 1679–1749* (University Park, PA:
Penn State University Press, 1994).

6. See, for example, David D. Hall, *Worlds of Wonder, Days of Judgment:
Popular Religious Belief in Early New England* (Cambridge, MA: Harvard
University Press, 1989).

7. Louise Breen, *Transgressing the Bounds: Subversive Enterprises
among the Puritan Elite in Massachusetts, 1630–1692* (New York: Oxford

University Press, 2001), 146–48, 166. Peter Silver has argued that proximity between groups led to more, not less fear (Silver, *Our Savage Neighbors: How Indian War Transformed Early America* [New York: Norton, 2008], xix).

8. Samuel Parris Sermon, September 11, 1692, quoted in Bryan F. Le Beau, *The Story of the Salem Witch Trials* (Saddle River, NJ: Prentice Hall, 1998), 189.

9. Thomas Maule, *Truth Held Forth and Maintained . . .* (New York: William Bradford, 1695), 185.

10. John Demos, *The Unredeemed Captive: A Family Story from Early America* (New York: Knopf, 1994).

11. Thomas S. Kidd, *The Great Awakening: The Roots of Evangelical Christianity in Colonial America* (New Haven, CT: Yale University Press, 2007), xvii.

12. Samuel Davies, "On the Defeat of General Braddock, 1755," quoted in Mark A. Noll, *America's God: From Jonathan Edwards to Abraham Lincoln* (New York: Oxford University Press, 2002), 91; Esther Edwards Burr to Sally Prince, August 8–9, 1755, *The Journal of Esther Edwards Burr*, ed. Carol Karlson and Laurie Crumpacker (New Haven, CT: Yale University Press, 1984), 142; Thomas Prince, *Extraordinary Events the Doings of God*, quoted in Kidd, *The Great Awakening*, 172. On the transference of anti-Catholic language to the English government during the American Revolution, see Nathan O. Hatch, *The Sacred Cause of Liberty: Republican Thought and the Millennium in Revolutionary America* (New Haven, CT: Yale University Press, 1977); Thomas Paine, *Common Sense* (Mineola, NY: Dover Thrift Edition, 1997), 12.

13. For a short introduction to this age of Christian reform, see John Fea, "Religion and Reform in the Early American Republic," in Jonathan Daniel Wells, ed., *The Routledge History of Nineteenth-Century America* (New York: Routledge, 2018), 62–73.

14. Lyman Beecher, *Plea for the West* (Cincinnati, OH: Truman and Smith, 1835), 9–10, 12, 47.

15. Beecher, *Plea for the West*, 66–68.

16. Beecher, *Plea for the West*, 68–69, 70, 72, 160.

17. Richard J. Carwardine, *Evangelicals and Politics in Antebellum*

America (New Haven, CT: Yale University Press, 1993), 321, 80, 210, 33, 129, 47.

18. "Know-Nothing Platform, 1856," *Wikisource*, last edited March 24, 2017, accessed December 16, 2017, https://en.wikisource.org/wiki/Know -Nothing_Platform_1856.

19. Carwardine, *Evangelicals and Politics*, 219–33; Tyler Anbinder, *Nativism and Slavery: The Northern Know Nothings and the Politics of the 1850s* (New York: Oxford University Press, 1992), 48–49.

20. See Eric R. Schlereth, *An Age of Infidels: The Politics of Religious Controversy in the Early United States* (Philadelphia: University of Pennsylvania Press, 2013).

21. Jonathan Den Hartog, *Patriotism and Piety: Federalist Politics and Religious Struggle in the New American Nation* (Charlottesville: University of Virginia Press, 2015).

22. Fea, *The Bible Cause*, 27–28.

23. Jedidiah Morse, *A Sermon, Delivered at the New North Church in Boston . . .* (Boston: Samuel Hall, 1798), 21, 26; Den Hartog, *Patriotism and Piety*, 45–55; Jedidiah Morse, *A Sermon Exhibiting the Present Dangers . . .* (Hartford, CT: Hudson and Goodwin, 1799).

24. Timothy Dwight, *The Duty of Americans, at the Present Crisis* (New Haven, CT: Thomas and Samuel Green, 1798), 1–13; Den Hartog, *Patriotism and Piety*, 40, 45, 50, 54, 55, 57, 59, 105.

25. For an overview of the election, see Edward J. Larson, *A Magnificent Catastrophe: The Tumultuous Election of 1800, America's First Presidential Campaign* (New York: Free Press, 2007).

26. William Linn, *Serious Considerations on the Election of a President* (Trenton, NJ: Sherman, Mersmon and Thomas, 1800), 4, 15, 16, 23.

27. Thomas Kidd, *God of Liberty: A Religious History of the American Revolution* (New York: Basic Books, 2012), 230.

28. Amanda Porterfield, *Conceived in Doubt: Religion and Politics in the New American Nation* (Chicago: University of Chicago Press, 2012), 16–17; Fea, *The Bible Cause*, 10, 28; Schlereth, *An Age of Infidels*, 49.

29. For a good discussion of the evangelical ethos of the antebellum South, see Luke Harlow, "The Long Life of Proslavery Religion," in Gregory P. Downs and Kate Masur, eds., *The World the Civil War Made* (Chapel Hill: University of North Carolina Press, 2015), 132–34.

30. Eugene Genovese, "Religion in the Collapse of the American Union," in Randall M. Miller, Harry S. Stout, and Charles Reagan Wilson, eds., *Religion and the American Civil War* (New York: Oxford University Press, 1998), 82.

31. Matthew Mason, *Slavery and Politics in the Early American Republic* (Chapel Hill: University of North Carolina Press, 2006), 108-19, 126; Carl Lawrence Paulus, *The Slaveholding Crisis: Fear of Insurrection and the Coming of the Civil War* (Baton Rouge: Louisiana State University Press, 2017).

32. Paulus, *The Slaveholding Crisis*, 21-24; Charles Irons, *The Origins of Proslavery Christianity: White and Black Evangelicals in Colonial and Antebellum Virginia* (Chapel Hill: University of North Carolina Press, 2014), 140. Also John Patrick Daly, *When Slavery Was Called Freedom: Evangelicalism, Proslavery, and the Causes of the Civil War* (Lexington: The University Press of Kentucky, 2002), 30-55.

33. Mitchell Snay, *Gospel of Disunion: Religion and Separatism in the Antebellum South* (New York: Cambridge University Press, 1993), 74; Paulus, *The Slaveholding Crisis*, 131-48.

34. Larry S. Tise has argued that about half of all proslavery pamphlets published in the United States were written by ministers (Tise, *Proslavery: A History of the Defense of Slavery in America, 1701-1840* [Athens: University of Georgia Press, 1987], xii).

35. Mark A. Noll, *America's God: From Jonathan Edwards to Abraham Lincoln* (New York: Oxford University Press, 1993), 388-89; Snay, *Gospel of Disunion*, 54-56; Thomas Dew, "An Essay on Slavery [1832]," in *The Pro-Slavery Argument: As Maintained by the Most Distinguished Writers of the Southern States* (Charleston, SC: Walker, Richards, 1852), 451-62.

36. Noll, "The Bible and Slavery," in *Religion and the Civil War*, 45-46; Luke Harlow, *Religion, Race, and the Making of Confederate Kentucky, 1830-1880* (New York: Cambridge University Press, 2014), 4-5.

37. Robert Dabney, *A Defence of Virginia: and through Her, of the South* (New York: E. J. Hale and Son, 1867), 203-4; Harlow, *Religion, Race, and the Making of Confederate Kentucky*, 117.

38. Genovese, "Religion in the Collapse of the American Union," 80; James H. Thornwell, "The Rights and the Duties of Masters," May 26, 1850, in David B. Cheesebrough, ed., *"God Ordained This War": Sermons on the Sectional Crisis, 1830-1865* (Columbia: University of South Carolina Press,

1991), 177–78; Benjamin Morgan Palmer, *Slavery a Divine Trust: The Duty of the South to Preserve and Perpetuate the Institution As It Now Exists* (New York: George F. Nesbitt & Co., 1861), 7, 12.

39. Harlow, *Religion, Race,* 123–25, 169; Snay, *Gospel of Disunion,* 93; Drew Gilpin Faust, *Mothers of Invention: Women of the Slaveholding South in the American Civil War* (Chapel Hill: University of North Carolina Press, 1996), 57; Charles B. Dew, *Apostles of Disunion* (Charlottesville: University of Virginia Press, 2001); Bruce Levin, *Confederate Emancipation: Southern Plans to Free and Arm Slaves during the Civil War* (New York: Oxford University Press, 2006), 49–50.

40. Harlow, *Religion, Race, and the Making of Confederate Kentucky,* 168–69; Paulus, *The Slaveholding Crisis,* 154–56.

41. R. L. Dabney, *Ecclesiastical Relation of Negroes* (Richmond, VA: Boys and Girls Monthly, 1868), 4, 6, 7, 8.

42. Mark Noll, *God and Race in American Politics* (Princeton, NJ: Princeton University Press, 2008), 75–76; Paul Harvey, *Freedom's Coming: Religious Culture and the Shaping of the South from the Civil War through the Civil Rights Era* (Chapel Hill: University of North Carolina Press, 2005); Ivan Evans, *Cultures of Violence: Racial Violence and the Origins of Segregation in South Africa and the American South* (Manchester, UK: University of Manchester Press, 2010), 133, 137, 153; Charles Reagan Wilson, *Baptized in the Blood: The Religion of the Lost Cause, 1865–1920* (Athens: University of Georgia Press, 1982), 82.

43. Nicholas Lemann, *Redemption: The Last Battle of the Civil War* (New York: Farrar, Straus and Giroux, 2006), 185.

44. Frances Fitzgerald, *The Evangelicals: The Struggle to Shape America* (New York: Simon and Schuster, 2017), 58–60.

45. These paragraphs draw heavily on material in John Fea, *Was America Founded as a Christian Nation? A Historical Introduction* (Louisville: Westminster John Knox, 2011), 43–47.

46. George Marsden, *Fundamentalism and American Culture: The Shaping of Twentieth-Century Evangelicalism, 1870–1925* (New York: Oxford University Press, 1980), 103, 134, 150–63, 207.

47. Marsden, *Fundamentalism and American Culture,* 17, 49, 191, 208; Matthew Sutton, *American Apocalypse: A History of Modern Evangelicalism* (Cambridge, MA: Harvard University Press, 2014), 179, 196–97, 207.

48. Sutton, *American Apocalypse*, 128, 130–35.

49. See Donald W. Dayton, *The Theological Roots of Pentecostalism* (Metuchen, NJ: Scarecrow Press, 1987); Marsden, *Fundamentalism and American Culture*, 72–101.

50. Mark A. Noll, *The Scandal of the Evangelical Mind* (Grand Rapids: Eerdmans, 1994).

51. Most recently, Brendan Pietsch, *Dispensational Modernism* (New York: Oxford University Press, 2015).

52. Doug Frank, *Less Than Conquerors: How Evangelicals Entered the Twentieth Century* (Grand Rapids: Eerdmans, 1986), 73, cited in Noll, *The Scandal of the Evangelical Mind*, 121.

53. See, for example, William V. Trollinger, *God's Empire: William Bell Riley and Midwestern Fundamentalism* (Madison: University of Wisconsin Press, 1991).

NOTES TO CHAPTER 4

1. C. Stephen Jaeger, *The Origins of Courtliness: Civilizing Trends and the Formation of Courtly Ideals, 939–1210* (Philadelphia: University of Pennsylvania Press, 1985), 54.

2. Keith Brown, *Noble Power in Scotland from the Reformation to the Revolution* (Edinburgh: Edinburgh University Press, 2011), 183–90; Baldesar Castiglione, *The Book of Courtier*, trans. George Bull (New York: Penguin Classics, 1976; originally published in 1528); Aldo Scaglione, *Knights at Court: Courtliness, Chivalry and Courtesy from Ottoman Germany to the Italian Renaissance* (Berkeley: University of California Press, 1992), 276; Jaeger, *The Origins of Courtliness*, 43–44, 58.

3. Jaeger, *The Origins of Courtliness*, 24, 58, 86.

4. Joachim Burke, *Courtly Culture: Literature and Society in the High Middle Ages* (Berkeley: University of California Press, 1991), 418.

5. John Fea, "Court Evangelical: We Have 'Unprecedented Access' to the Trump White House," *The Way of Improvement Leads Home*, August 2, 2017, https://thewayofimprovement.com/2017/08/02/court -evangelical-we-have-unprecedented-access-to-the-trump-white -house/; "Paula White Says Opposition to President Trump Is Opposition

to God," Right Wing Watch, August 21, 2017, https://www.youtube.com/watch?time_continue=1&v=STcgXcxOhNc.

6. The August 18, 2017, video interview with A. R. Bernard is available in the article "Pastor First to Quit Trump's Evangelical Advisory Board: 'There Was a Line,'" CNN, updated August 20, 2017, https://www.youtube.com/watch?v=c3EUrTzzP78.

7. Samuel Smith, "Greg Laurie Details White House Dinner with Evangelicals, Trump Breaking Protocol," *Christian Post*, May 8, 2017, https://www.christianpost.com/news/greg-laurie-details-white-house-dinner-with-evangelicals-trump-breaking-protocol-182938/.

8. "President Trump Declares National Day of Prayer for Harvey Victims," C-Span on YouTube, September 1, 2017, https://www.youtube.com/watch?v=9sEZpgwdKzE.

9. "God and Donald Trump and Let Trump Be Trump," C-SPAN, December 8, 2017, https://www.c-span.org/video/?437899-2/god-donald-trump-let-trump-trump.

10. Jerry Falwell Jr. interview with Jeanine Pirro, Fox News on YouTube, July 1, 2017, https://www.youtube.com/watch?v=sn_HtO7CDno.

11. Dr. Robert Jeffress on Lou Dobbs Tonight, Fox Business on YouTube, August 18, 2017, https://www.youtube.com/watch?v=U9Kqc-IrGqA.

12. Bruce Henderson, "Evangelical Leader Stays on Trump Advisory Council Despite Charlottesville Response," *Charlotte Observer*, August 24, 2017, http://www.charlotteobserver.com/news/local/article169163722.html.

13. Johnnie Moore, "Evangelical Trump Adviser: Why I Won't Bail on the White House," *Religion News Service*, August 24, 2017, http://religionnews.com/2017/08/24/johnnie-moore-why-i-wont-bail-on-the-white-house/.

14. Kate Shellnutt, "Should Christians Keep Advising a President They Disagree With?" *Christianity Today*, September 6, 2017, http://www.christianitytoday.com/news/2017/september/should-christians-keep-advising-president-they-disagree-wit.html.

15. Nina Burleigh, "Does God Believe in Trump? White Evangelicals Are Sticking with Their 'Prince of Lies,'" *Newsweek*, October 5, 2017, http://www.newsweek.com/2017/10/13/donald-trump-white

-evangelicals-support-god-677587.html; Stephen Mansfield, *Choosing Donald Trump* (Grand Rapids: Baker, 2017), 94–95.

16. Sarah Pulliam Bailey, "'God Is Not Against Building Walls!' The Sermon Trump Heard from Robert Jeffress before His Inauguration," *Washington Post*, January 20, 2017, https://www .washingtonpost.com/news/acts-of-faith/wp/2017/01/20/god-is-not -against-building-walls-the-sermon-donald-trump-heard-before -his-inauguration/?utm_term=.4c40c927266f.

17. See John Fea, *Was America Founded as a Christian Nation? A Historical Introduction* (Louisville: Westminster John Knox Press, 2011; rev. ed., 2015).

18. "Jerry Falwell Jr.: 'Evangelicals Have Found Their Dream President,'" *Sojourners*, April 30, 2017, https://sojo.net/articles/jerry-falwell-jr -evangelicals-have-found-their-dream-president.

19. John Fea, "Jerry Falwell Jr. Endorses Donald Trump," *The Way of Improvement Leads Home*, January 19, 2016, https://thewayofimprovement .com/2016/01/19/jerry-falwell-jr-endorses-donald-trump/.

20. "To Elect Godly Leaders, Evangelicals in U.S. Politics," *Interfaith Voices*, May 26, 2016, http://interfaithradio.org/Archive/2016-May/To_ Elect_Godly_Leaders__Evangelicals_in_U_S__Politics.

21. "Dr. Robert Jeffress and Peter Wehner Join Mike for Important Debate over Evangelical Christian Support of Trump," The Mike Gallagher Show, July 12, 2016, http://www.mikeonline.com/dr-robertjeffress -peter_wehner-join-mike-for-an-important-debate-over-evangelical -christians-support-of-trump/.

22. For a helpful introduction to these matters, see Ronald J. Sider, *The Scandal of Evangelical Politics* (Grand Rapids: Baker, 2008), 28–32.

23. Robert Jeffress, *Twilight's Last Gleaming: How America's Last Days Can Be Your Best Days* (Brentwood, TN: Worthy Publishing, 2011), 18, 29, 30–31.

24. Jeffress, *Twilight's Last Gleaming*, 103–8.

25. Jeffress, *Twilight's Last Gleaming*, 18, 30, 71.

26. Brad Christerson and Richard Flory, *The Rise of Network Christianity* (New York: Oxford University Press, 2017).

27. Christerson and Flory, *The Rise of Network Christianity*, 91–104.

28. John Fea, "Ted Cruz's Campaign Is Fueled by a Dominionist Vision

for America," *Washington Post*, February 4, 2016, https://www.washington post.com/national/religion/ted-cruzs-campaign-is-fueled-by-a -dominionist-vision-for-america-commentary/2016/02/04/86373158 -cb6a-11e5-b9ab-26591104bb19_story.html?utm_term=.edbfaa648ab5; Christerson and Flory, *The Rise of Network Christianity*, 127.

29. Steven Strang interview with Mike Bickle, "How Trump's Presidency Could Open Doors to a Great Awakening in America," Strang Report Podcast on Charisma Podcast Network, accessed December 30, 2017, https://www.cpnshows.com/shows/strangreport/fc7a069a62cbb 74d1d4bb844d25f60b7.

30. Steven Strang interview with Lance Wallnau, "Is Donald Trump America's Cyrus?" The Strang Report Podcast on Charisma Podcast Network, accessed December 30, 2017, https://www.charismapodcast network.com/shows/strangreport/fa261ca761fb800f76c6804ed34998f5. Many INC prophets and their followers have built a popular online presence at the website The Elijah's List, www.elijahlist.com.

31. Steven Strang, *God and Donald Trump* (Lake Mary, FL: Frontline, 2017), 40–41; Steven Strang interview with Cindy Jacobs, "Trump Election an Answer to 'Urgent, Pentecostal-Type Prayer,'" Strang Report Podcast on Charisma Podcast Network, accessed December 30, 2017, https://www .cpnshows.com/shows/strangreport/9d553fafob6c883454100a45dff94cf1.

32. The most thorough examination of the POTUS Shield movement is Peter Montgomery, "POTUS Shield: Trump's Dominionist Prayer Warriors and the 'Prophetic Order of the United States,'" Right Wing Watch, August 2017, http://www.rightwingwatch.org/report/potus -shield-trumps-dominionist-prayer-warriors-and-the-prophetic-order -of-the-united-states/. Also Sunnivie Brydum, "A President 'Anointed by God': POTUS Shield and Religious Right's Affair with Trump," *Religion Dispatches*, August 4, 2017, http://religiondispatches.org/a-president -anointed-by-god-potus-shield-and-religious-rights-affair-with -trump/.

33. Kate Bowler, *Blessed: A History of the American Prosperity Gospel* (New York: Oxford University Press, 2013), 7, 11, 74, 75, 137. Also Phillip Luke Sinitiere, *Salvation with a Smile: Joel Osteen, Lakewood Church, and American Christianity* (New York: New York University Press, 2015).

34. Shayne Lee and Phillip Luke Sinitiere, *Holy Mavericks: Evan-*

gelical Innovators and the Spiritual Marketplace (New York: New York University Press, 2009), 111, 113, 124, 125; Michael Horton, "Evangelicals Should Be Deeply Troubled by Donald Trump's Attempt to Mainstream Heresy," *Washington Post*, January 3, 2017, https://www.washington post.com/news/acts-of-faith/wp/2017/01/03/evangelicals-should-be -deeply-troubled-by-donald-trumps-attempt-to-mainstream-heresy /?utm_term=.37727378557d.

35. Lee and Sinitiere, *Holy Mavericks*, 119, 121; Bowler, *Blessed*, 168, 169; Horton, "Evangelicals"; Kate Shellnutt, "The Story behind Donald Trump's Controversial Prayer Partner," *Christianity Today*, January 19, 2017, http://www.christianitytoday.com/ct/2017/january-web-only/ paula-white-donald-trump-prayer-partner-inauguration.html; Leo-nardo Blair, "Televangelist Paula White Hawks 'Resurrection Life' for $1,144 'Seed,'" *Christian Post*, April 19, 2016, https://www.christianpost .com/news/televangelist-paula-white-hawks-resurrection-life-1144 -dollar-seed-162088/.

36. Lee and Sinitiere, *Holy Mavericks*, 111; Emily McFarlan Miller, "Prosperity, Heresy and Trump: Inauguration Pastor Paula White Answers Her Critics," Religion News Service, January 19, 2017, http://religionnews.com/2017/01/19/prosperity-heresy-and-trump -inauguration-pastor-paula-white-answers-her-critics/.

37. Bowler, *Blessed*, 55–68; Gwenda Blair, "How Norman Vin-cent Peale Taught Donald Trump to Worship Himself," *Politico*, Oc-tober 6, 2015, https://www.politico.com/magazine/story/2015/10/ donald-trump-2016-norman-vincent-peale-213220.

38. Stanley Hauerwas and Jonathan Tran, "A Sanctuary Politics: Be-ing the Church in the Time of Trump," ABC Religion & Ethics, March 31, 2017, http://www.abc.net.au/religion/articles/2017/03/30/4645538.htm.

39. Thomas Berg, "Does This New Bill Threaten California Christian Colleges' Religious Freedom?" *Christianity Today*, July 5, 2016, http:// www.christianitytoday.com/ct/2016/july-web-only/california-sb-1146 -religious-freedom.html. Eventually the bill was amended and Biola and other California Christian colleges were able to support it. See Evan Low and Barry H. Corey, "We First Battled over LGBT and Reli-gious Rights. Here's How We Became Unlikely Friends," *Washington Post*, March 3, 2017, https://www.washingtonpost.com/news/acts-of

-faith/wp/2017/03/03/we-first-battled-over-lgbt-and-religious-rights
-heres-how-we-became-unlikely-friends/?utm_term=.cd1d3f6ed15b.

40. "Falwell Clarifies Federal Aid Benefactors," *Liberty News*, August 17, 2011, http://www.liberty.edu/index.cfm?PID=18495&MID=35605.

41. Elizabeth Schmidt, "How Much Does the Johnson Amendment Curtail Church Freedom?" *Real Clear Religion*, February 21, 2017, http://www.realclearreligion.org/articles/2017/02/21/how_much_does_the_johnson_amendment_curtail_church_freedom_110115.html.

42. Stephen Mansfield, *Choosing Donald Trump* (Grand Rapids: Baker, 2017), 101–8.

43. Derek Hawkins, "Critics Said Trump's 'Religious Liberty' Order Does Nothing," *Washington Post*, August 25, 2017, https://www.washingtonpost.com/news/morning-mix/wp/2017/08/25/critics-said-trumps-religious-liberty-order-does-nothing-the-administrations-lawyers-seem-to-agree/?hpid=hp_hp-morning-mix_mm-liberty%3Ahomepage%2Fstory&utm_term=.73f665da5d7e.

44. John Fea, "The Evangelical Courtiers Who Kneel before the President's Feet," Religion News Service, May 12, 2017, http://religionnews.com/2017/05/12/the-evangelical-courtiers-who-kneel-before-the-presidents-feet/.

45. Carol Pipes, "Majority of Pastors Disapprove of Pulpit Endorsements," *Lifeway Research*, October 1, 2012, http://www.lifeway.com/Article/research-majority-pastors-disapprove-pulpit-endorsements.

46. "Trump's Evangelical Base Is Ecstatic over Jerusalem Decision," Fox News on YouTube, December 7, 2017, https://www.youtube.com/watch?v=OYdXmY60904.

47. Chris Mitchell, "'I See Us in the Middle of Prophecy!,'" *CBN News*, December 10, 2017, http://www1.cbn.com/cbnnews/israel/2017/december/mike-evans-we-rsquo-re-in-the-middle-of-prophecy.

48. Grant Wacker, *America's Pastor: Billy Graham and the Shaping of a Nation* (Cambridge, MA: Harvard University Press, 2014), 204–12; Steven P. Miller, *Billy Graham and the Rise of the Republican South* (Philadelphia: University of Pennsylvania Press), 69–84.

49. Miller, *Billy Graham*, 126, 127, 130, 141.

50. Wacker, *America's Pastor*, 212–14; Miller, *Billy Graham*, 184, 187.

51. Cal Thomas and Ed Dobson, *Blinded by Might: Can the Religious Right Save America?* (Grand Rapids: Zondervan, 1999), 12, 17.

52. Thomas and Dobson, *Blinded by Might*, 23–27.

53. Thomas and Dobson, *Blinded by Might*, 49, 53, 54, 87, 96.

54. See David Kuo, *Tempted by Faith: An Inside Story of Political Seduction* (New York: Free Press, 2006).

55. Kuo, *Tempted by Faith*, 168, 169.

56. Kuo, *Tempted by Faith*, 73, 229–30, 250.

NOTES TO CHAPTER 5

1. John Fea, *Was America Founded as a Christian Nation? A Historical Introduction* (Louisville: Westminster John Knox, 2011). The above paragraphs draw heavily from "Was America Founded as a Christian Nation?" a CNN roundtable hosted by historian Mark Edwards. Edwards, "Was America Founded as a Christian Nation?" CNN, July 4, 2015, http://www.cnn.com/2015/07/02/living/america-christian-nation/index.html.

2. Svetlana Boym, *The Future of Nostalgia* (New York: Basic Books, 2001), xiii, xiv.

3. Robert Jeffress, "America Is a Christian Nation," sermon preached June 17, 2017, at First Baptist Church—Dallas, https://www.oneplace.com/ministries/pathway-to-victory/listen/america-is-a-christian-nation-part-1-536068.html.

4. Jeffress, "America Is a Christian Nation."

5. For an introduction to Barton, see John Fea, *Was America Founded as a Christian Nation?* (Louisville: Westminster John Knox, 2015 rev. ed.), 247–49. See also Warren Throckmorton and Michael Coulter, *Getting Jefferson Right: Fact Checking Claims about Our Third President* (Grove City, PA: Salem Grove Press, 2012); John Fea, "David Barton: 'Trump Is God's Guy,'" *The Way of Improvement Leads Home*, June 30, 2016, https://thewayofimprovement.com/2016/06/30/david-barton-trump-is-gods-guy/; Kyle Mantyla, "David Barton Advocates Seven Mountains Dominionism," *Right Wing Watch*, April 4, 2011, http://www.rightwingwatch.org/post/david-barton-advocates-seven-mountains-dominionism/.

6. For a powerful statement on the idolatry of Christian nationalism, see Gregory Boyd, *The Myth of a Christian Nation* (Grand Rapids: Zonder-

van, 2005); see also Richard T. Hughes, *Christian America and the Kingdom of God* (Champaign: University of Illinois Press), 2009.

7. Glenn Tinder, *The Political Meaning of Christianity: An Interpretation* (Baton Rouge: Louisiana State University Press, 1989), 55, 58, 61, 134, 242. On the relationship between Christian hope, the resurrection, the new heaven, and the new earth, see N. T. Wright, *Surprised by Hope: Rethinking Heaven, the Resurrection, and the Mission of the Church* (New York: HarperOne, 2008).

8. Tinder, *Political Meaning of Christianity*, 102.

9. Quoted in Yoni Appelbaum, "Why There Was a Civil War," *The Atlantic*, May 1, 2017, https://www.theatlantic.com/politics/archive/2017/05/why-there-was-a-civil-war/524925/.

10. See, e.g., Christopher Wilson, "Historians React to Trump's Civil War Comments: That's Entirely Wrong in Every Respect," *Yahoo News*, May 1, 2017, https://www.yahoo.com/news/historians-react-trumps-civil-war-comments-thats-entirely-wrong-every-respect-181325014.html.

11. Jose A. Del Real, "Trump, Pivoting to the General Election, Hones 'America First' Foreign Policy Vision," *Washington Post*, April 27, 2016, https://www.washingtonpost.com/news/post-politics/wp/2016/04/27/trump-pivoting-to-the-general-election-hones-america-first-foreign-policy-vision/?utm_term=.87c401cfbce1; "Trump Transcript: 'America First' Security Speech," *Al Jazeera*, December 18, 2017, http://www.aljazeera.com/news/2017/12/trump-transcript-america-security-speech-171218205011166.html.

12. Susan Dunn, "Trump's 'America First' Has Ugly Echoes from U.S. History," CNN, April 28, 2016, http://www.cnn.com/2016/04/27/opinions/trump-america-first-ugly-echoes-dunn/index.html; Krishnadev Calamur, "A Short History of 'America First,'" *The Atlantic*, January 21, 2017, https://www.theatlantic.com/politics/archive/2017/01/trump-america-first/514037/.

13. Ron Elving, "Trump Vows Policy Vision of 'America First,'" NPR, January 21, 2017, https://www.npr.org/2017/01/21/510877650/trump-vows-policy-vision-of-america-first-recalling-phrases-controversial-past; Louisa Thomas, "America First, for Charles Lindbergh and Donald Trump," *The New Yorker*, July 24, 2016, https://www.newyorker.com/

news/news-desk/america-first-for-charles-lindbergh-and-donald
-trump.

14. Maeve Reston, "How Trump's Deportation Plan Failed 62 Years
Ago," CNN, January 19, 2016, http://www.cnn.com/2016/01/19/politics/
donald-trump-deportation-mexico-eisenhower/index.html.

15. John Nevins, *Operation Gatekeeper: The Rise of the "Illegal Alien"
and the Making of the U.S.-Mexico Boundary* (New York: Routledge, 2002),
28–29.

16. Mae M. Ngai, *Impossible Subjects: Illegal Aliens and the Making of
Modern America* (Princeton, NJ: Princeton University Press, 2004), 155–56.

17. Louis Nelson, "Trump: 'I Am the Law and Order Candidate,'" *Politico*, July 11, 2016, https://www.politico.com/story/2016/07/trump-law
-order-candidate-225372.

18. Dan Roberts and Ben Jacobs, "Donald Trump Proclaims Himself
'Law and Order' Candidate at Republican Convention," *The Guardian*, July
22, 2016, https://www.theguardian.com/us-news/2016/jul/21/donald
-trump-republican-national-convention-speech.

19. Michael W. Flamm, *Law and Order: Street Crime, Civil Unrest, and
the Crisis of Liberalism in the 1960s* (New York: Columbia University Press,
2005).

20. Tali Mendelberg, *The Race Card: Campaign Strategy, Implicit Mes-
sages, and the Norm of Equality* (Princeton, NJ: Princeton University Press,
2001), 96–98.

21. Michael Gerson, "Trump's Attack on John Lewis Is the Essence of
Narcissism," *Washington Post*, January 15, 2017, https://www.washington
post.com/opinions/trumps-attack-on-john-lewis-is-the-essence-of
-narcissism/2017/01/15/7e3d9ab6-db4d-11e6-ad42-f3375f271c9c_story
.html?utm_term=.6ef68ef6ca6d.

22. Sam Wineburg, *Historical Thinking and Other Unnatural Acts*
(Philadelphia: Temple University Press, 2001), 24.

NOTES TO THE CONCLUSION

1. One of the best examples is John Inazu, *Confident Pluralism: Surviving and Thriving through Deep Difference* (Chicago: University of Chicago
Press, 2016).

2. I recorded some of my thoughts on the "Returning to the Roots of the Civil Rights" bus tour. See John Fea, "Episode 28: That Memphis Sound," *The Way of Improvement Leads Home*, October 29, 2017, https:// thewayofimprovement.com/category/civil-rights-bus-tour-june-2017/.

3. Christopher Lasch, *The True and Only Heaven: Progress and Its Critics* (New York: W. W. Norton, 1991), 80–81.

4. Glenn Tinder, *The Fabric of Hope: An Essay* (Atlanta: Scholars Press, 1999), 13.

5. James Davison Hunter, *To Change the World: The Irony, Tragedy, and Possibility of Christianity in the Late Modern World* (New York: Oxford University Press, 2010), 253.

6. On the civil rights movement as a religious revival, see David Chappel, *A Stone of Hope: Prophetic Religion and the Death of Jim Crow* (Chapel Hill: University of North Carolina Press, 2004), 74, 87–104; Lasch, *True and Only Heaven*, 378, 390.

7. Martin Luther King Jr., "Letter from a Birmingham Jail," *Christian Century*, June 12, 1963, 773.

INDEX

Abernathy, Ralph, 181
abolitionism, 98–99, 100, 101–3
abortion: court evangelicals'
    political agenda, 139, 180;
    Hillary Clinton and pro-choice
    position, 71–72; Obama and
    pro-choice position, 23–24; *Roe
    v. Wade*, 27, 55–56, 57–58, 61,
    122, 138–39, 148; and Trump's
    Supreme Court nominations,
    66, 138
Access Hollywood tape, 4, 67, 120
Adams, John, 15, 69, 95–96, 156–57
Affordable Care Act (ACA), 5,
    23–24, 40
African Americans: civil rights
    movement, 46, 47, 54–55, 181–
    90; early twentieth-century
    fundamentalists' racism and,
    101–2; and evangelical racism
    in the Civil War–era South,
    97–104; Rev. Wright on past

treatment of, 21–22. *See also*
    racism
The Age of Reason (Paine), 97
*The Age of Revelation, or the Age
    of Reason Shewn to Be an Age of
    Infidelity* (Boudinot), 97
Ahn, Che, 129
Al-Assad, Bashar, 39
Amedia, Frank, 133
America First Committee, 171–72
"America First" foreign policy, 5,
    165–66, 171–72
American Bible Society, 52, 97
anti-Semitism, 147, 171
Ashcroft, John, 150
Assemblies of God, 36, 129
Augustine, Saint, 125–26

Bachman, Michelle, 19, 65, 132
Bacote, Vincent, 32–33
Bader-Saye, Scott, 43
Bakker, Jim, 118, 134
Bakker, Tammy, 134

early twentieth-century fundamentalists and, 104–5; *Everson* decision and busing of Catholic students, 48; mid-twentieth century, 49–50; and New England Puritans, 84–85; Protestant anti-Catholicism and fears of, 15, 49–50, 84–92, 107–8

Charisma (magazine), 132

Charleston church shooting (June 2015), 20–21

Charlottesville white suprem-acist riots (August 2017), 119, 120–21, 166

Christerson, Brad, 129

Christian Broadcasting Network, 144

Christian Century, 49

Christian Coalition, 61

Christianity Today, 40, 51, 56

Christian Right, 57–64, 123–29; and control of Supreme Court, 61, 66; and court evangelicals, 123–29; culture-war playbook and the emergence of, 57–64, 202n21; the Moral Majority, 8, 34, 60, 147–49; opposition to desegregation, 9, 202n21; reaction to Bill Clinton, 62–64, 66, 69, 124; Republican Party and the 1980 Republican platform, 60; wing of American evangel-icalism, 59, 123–29

Christian Zionists, 144

Churchill, Winston, 171

Church of God (Cleveland, Ten-nessee), 129

Church of God in Christ, 129

Church of the Holy Trinity v. United States (1892), 161

Civil Rights Act (1964), 54, 176

civil rights movement, 46, 47, 54–55, 181–90; freedom riders, 182, 185; history (not nostal-gia), 188–90; hope (not fear), 182–85; humility (not political power), 185–88; a 2017 histor-ical bus tour through sites of, 182; white evangelicals and, 54–55

Civil War, 97–104, 166; evan-gelical racism and politics of fear in American South, 97–104; postwar challenges to traditional evangelical beliefs, 104–6; Southern defense of slavery, 97–104; Trump on Andrew Jackson and, 167

Clement, Kim, 131

Clinton, Bill: on abortion, 23, 62; and Billy Graham, 145; and the Christian Right, 60, 62–64, 66, 69–70, 124; Defense of Marriage Act (DOMA), 25; Lewinsky affair, 62–64, 70

Clinton, Hillary: evangelicals and, 70–73; as First Lady, 62, 70; and Lewinsky affair, 70; "Pizzagate" conspiracy theory, 17; pro-choice position, 72, 138; and religious liberty issues, 72; and 2016 presidential cam-paign, 6, 17, 38, 41, 68, 70–73

The Clinton Chronicles (film), 62

College of New Jersey (Prince-ton), 86

College of William and Mary (Williamsburg, Virginia), 100

INDEX

INDEX

INDEX

INDEX